Verses in Inner City Scriptures (& Essays from Concrete Sandlots)

given this book

given to Dr. Burnece Pulliam

From: Kevin A. Williams

on 08/31/2020

CREDITS

Ellen, Blanche, Golden, and Willie Sr. are the 4 corners of my universe, my foundation, the pillars of my world, without them or their memories, K.A. Williams does not exist.

Dedications:

This is the first poetry book ever featuring K.A. Williams. I write poetry and not spoken word, because spoken word is such a hip thing and when it's all said and done, I am a poet and proud of it. Also please buy my book because I have a very big 2 year old nephew and a cool niece and a bunch of God kids who need things in life that only with your generous support can they attain. Real quick, I am a city guy who is learning to appreciate the country way of life. I often tell people my two favorite cities in the world are Chicago and Austin, TX. When it's time for this Professor of Soul to call it a day, I might mosey on down 35 South to the ATX, hang out with Brian and Herman, make some Easy Livings, grill and talk garbage about everything and nothing. Or I might just go back home and hangout with Sam and Dave, get a turkey hoagy, my shoes shined at K & J and make power moves. Yet the third option is trying to find my brother Keyth, and his son Little Keyth something to eat as they rampage through food stores in a never ending quest to fill their gullet as my Mother talks about her "baby". Anyway space is money so let me begin thanking people in different sections. Also real quick, TBP means "The Black Prince", YFBG means "Your Favorite Black Guy", POS means "Professor of Soul", and the 11th & 1st Letter Future Kids Foundation is exactly that.

Roots: Ellen & Willie Williams Sr., Blanche & Golden Sylvester Tillman, Sylester & W. Bill Williams Jr., (my Grandparents and parents). Without any of these 6 people TBP would not be here now so big up's to God and this great group of people. Aunt Loretta, Cynthia, Alexis, Earline Evans, Mrs. DuBois, Deloris, Rosemary, Mrs. Mendenhall, Mrs. Mays, Mrs. Francis, Karen, Mrs. H. . These are my Aunts, my sister, and other women who have influenced me said a kind word or came into my life in a different fashion. Karen is my older sister and she never lets me forget it, always got me in mind. Loretta, Cynthia, are my mother's sister and by extension my other mothers. Alexis was probably one of my first heroine's in life, the smartest person I have ever met, the one who I was always intimidated to talk too, or just marveled at, saying she is brilliant is not enough. Mrs. Evans, Mendenhall, Mays, DuBois, Francis are the mothers of my soul brothers, they looked out for me, I ate over their homes, spent inordinate amounts of time over there, came to them for advice and in the case of Mrs. Mendenhall she was always that voice of compassion, Mrs. DuBois was cool, and Mrs. Evans she always kept it real, never allowed me to get too big, made sure I knew she was watching Brad and myself. Mrs. H. is the mother of someone from Teague, Baton Rogue, and Dallas I know who means a lot to TBP. All of these women have been there for yours truly.

Hudson, John, Jamel, Norman, Chuck, Andrew "Jackie", LeRoy, Mr. Francis, Tony Sr., Mr. Mendenhall, Mr. Evans, Mr. DuBois, Reggie, AJ, AD, Emil, Tim, Donnie, Mike, Moon, Richard, Duck, Charlie, Gerald, Sonny, Stan, Floyd, Ernie, Mike Lieteau, Mr. Curry, all men who influenced me, not a rogue's gallery but a pantheon of heroes. I never had to go far to find heroes, never had to read about great men, because I saw one every day. Thank you for being you, for never hiding what a real man looks like, teaching the game, making sure we were schooled to the streets, and recognized life.

Dylester, Myrtis, Hudson, Terrace, Sam, Dave, Cassandra, Cypriana, Ines, Jesse, Robin, Holly, Jason, Lauren T., Lauren C., Valencia, Rochelle, Tanya, Luvie, Tony, Torriante, Bianca, Erica, Golden, Nikki, Rikia, Jalen, Darryl, Kendrick, Malik, and all the rest. Thank you for being my cousins, for being an incredible extended family. I have more cousins than I could possibly name and I mean just 1st and 2nd cousins so if I forgot you, blame my head and not my heart.

Legal Team- Equator, Rob, Mike, George, thanks. EQ, the sister I never had, my confidant, my conscience, the one with that edge, Mike always a friend., Rob thanks, and George where the heck are you??

Sister friends-Dr. Callie Hall, LaLove, Kim, Jeanine, Geneen, Janeen, Lia, Barbara, Fern, Jennifer, Libby, Andrea, Genee (my unofficial editor who worked diligently through out the years encouraging me, cussing me out editing and re-editing), Sherry, Sylvia, Andrea, Inertia, Lori, Valerie (where are you) Wanda, Candy, Tonia, Lia, Brenda, Crystal, Mo Browne, June, Erica, all sister friends who are great people and mean the

6

world to me. Equator thanks for keeping me out of trouble, Callie for high school and college and Barb Barb for the many Springfield/Decatur adventures of your surrogate brother. Kim and Love thanks for being talented writers and in my corner, Jackie and Tonia for being prayer partners and your faith. Sonya Roberts, my photographer/illustrator/movie buddy, thank you very much for your diligence, dedication, and work ethic; I cannot compensate you enough for this project so I hope my thanks is enough!!!

Steps on my journey-what that means are sisters who helped me to grow as a man, and vice-versa. Jennifer, Camille (a great lawyer and good person, who hates the restless leg syndrome), Christal (seems like only yesterday at the ESPN zone, or Gladys late night dining), Jackie Slaughter (my Bluegrass Belle, with a heart like gold) Anika James, (one of the most mature women I have ever met in life, just a season too early) Keisha, Gina, Tammy, Paula (Doc you are awright in my book take care), LaShaun (a beautiful sister who has tenacity and poise, Etta James and the BET was one of the best gifts you ever gave me thank you for being you). Each of you guys were special in my life at various junctures, no regrets and I thank you, if I learned anything in life it is what Emil Jones taught me, "in most instances in life there is no such thing as a permanent friend or a permanent enemy, only permanent interest" so always stay interested in a brother doing right and the same to each of you, some people live by clichés I don't know what the future holds but I know it is brighter because of each of you.

Real quick the cats who keep a brother looking fresh from coast to coast, Dee and his Pops "Tom" from Catron's/Tom's on 111th & Western on the fabled Southside of Chicago, Danny's on 119th, Kevin in Austin, my guy Fly Ty in Dallas, and the 4 Wise Men, Relly, Old School, Wayne, and 'Sheed, from Relly's shop in Irving, Texas. These guys keep me looking like fresh and clean, dispense wisdom, get the low down from the streets, and make me feel welcome, how about a cut on the house every now and then !!!

My Crew- Sam, Dave, Keyth my brother and the one responsible for "The Big Guy", Eric, Rod, Brad, Mel, Bryant, Kevin M., Thomas, Mike P., Richard, Brian, Kendrick, Herman, Kevin S., Sherman, Andre, Brian F., Trevis, Joe, Jay, Swann, Popcorn, Chris, Mike S., Dre, Joseph, Marvin, Tory, Marquis, Craige, Craig, Aaron, LaDarryl, Mark, Terry, Chris, EV, Main, Rich, Stan, Akil, Maurice, Tim, Mohammed, DB, Keith, and all my guys from K.S.E.K.O.K. Larry, Billy, Jamie, Ernest, Chaz, DJ, Will, Angel, Torri, Chris, Kirk, Quan, Mike, Stan, Ron, thanks for keeping it real. Sam, Dave, Mel, Eric, Bryant, Brad, Kevin I have been knowing you forever and then some and thank you for keeping it real, and at times real ignorant. We have hustled from coast to coast, broke a lot of hearts along the way and still we managed to avoid prosecution by any law enforcement agencies and have only been banned in a few upscale joints. Remember an indictment is not a crime, only a conviction counts. Brian and Marquis, one of you Mothers got me down to Texas and the other one adopted me once I got here, you are both my two favorite Omega's (that isn't saying a lot). The brothers of Kappa Alpha Psi Chicago Alumni Chapter, and P.H.A.. Phoenix Lodge, Dre, Uncle Charlie, Trevis, and everyone I love you guys. DJ you are an Alpha and Mike T., and Mike P. are both Sigma's and I still like you guys !!!

DATING

Black folks and dating Intro

I wrote the following pieces because I am at the point in life that I am realizing that while life is grand it would be better if we were candid about certain things. Granted we are not going to be totally candid in every aspect of our lives, if a police officer asks if we ran that red light the answer is typically no, if the ball goes out on me in a close pick up game of basketball the answer has a high probability of being no or "I am not sure", if my Mother asks me if I enjoyed liver and onions the answer is going to be a yes (even at my age self preservation is a must because my Mother still throws a mean right hook). I wrote that because I enjoy meeting various ladies from different walks of life as I enjoy this dating phase of being over 30, but one thing that bugs me out is how many of my peers assume that status equates class or grace.

Honestly, I am not broaching any new territory, the Good Book tells us there is nothing new under the sun, there is nothing new we are just spins off the old. Yet, it amazes me that the more we learn, the more we earn, the more we prosper the more we fail. I know a brother who is a church going, Bible thumping guy, the sisters love him, yet if they knew his character that he was a chump, that he went after his friends girls, that he tried to force himself on a young lady I knew under the guise that they were having a prayer meeting, people would be amazed and before someone says "K.A. hates the church" stop it's not true, I believe in Christ and attend church, what I am tired of is the age old hypocrisy game. We are all hypocrites in some shape manner or form, the choice is when we impact others. The same goes for a friend of mine who sold mad drugs in the neighborhood the same guy who sits up and talks about how our country is destroying other countries while he tools around with Versace shades and a fly car sitting on 20 inch rims.

I meet sisters who are more educated than all our generations prior and they are in shape financially, but are so bankrupt spiritually. More in love with the aesthetics of a man than who a man is, not understanding that a lot of sisters want that superstar brother, the one who has multiple degrees, or a fly whip, or is a pro athlete, or is handsome, or has a lot of money, so what if this man is being bombarded by all these types of sisters, I asked some of them what makes you think you are going to stand out? Why wouldn't you be another notch on his belt? Another skin on the wall? Unless you are doing tricks in the bedroom that would rival Houdini you may be chasing a fantasy.

This is where the contradiction comes in, because at the same time I will say there are some good brothers out there, some guys who are outstanding. I was at dinner with some beautiful sisters recently and they were lamenting how there was a dearth of good black men, as they scanned the bar, and here I am sitting right next to them, as there eyes scanned and they locked on the same guy (though Fern disagrees). Now I am sitting thinking the next phrase will be that there are not enough good men, but rather than talk, meet engage, get to know a guy who is a good guy right next to them, they sought the same guy and guess what no one met him at all !!!!

Yes some of you will say, well "K.A. is so full of it, and he does not understand" but I do understand and over stand also. Think about it like this, there is one shiny new car with all the features a person wants and there are people who want that car and they all have a key. No one knows which key fits but they are all willing to try their keys, meanwhile there are 4 other 4 cars, maybe not as shiny, or maybe with a better engine under the hood but these cars may never be driven because the 4 people who have keys that don't fit lament about the car they missed out on, a crude analogy but you get my point. Awright back to my poetry.

If They Ever Asked

If they opened up the book of my soul and looked at the scroll it
would find a chapter emblazoned with your name on it
If they examined my brain they would find a region with your
name on it
Some have demarcations scrawled on their body in honor of
those who are special in their lives and respective eyes,
Mine is visible but yet unseen
Only the beholder and I know the source of the fresh writing
The Koran states that women are our fields and we are to go
into them
The Bible tells us that woman came from man's rib
And alludes to the fact that man must have his "missing" rib in
order to be whole
Sometimes in the shadow of the sun I see a silhouette that I bet
is yours
Sometimes when traipsing through our journey of life I feel your
presence even when you are not behind unopened doors
In anticipation I wait exhale inhale breathe deep in your nuance
that permeates my soul
When I glimpse you it is as if the sun has decided to kiss me, as
if the wind has been stilled
As if the earth has decided to revolve on its axis to our rhythm
As if the sun and moon, have come together in union to grant us
a moment not day and not yet night
But that happy medium that is only attained in memory of
childhood days
When lips join in that brief but fulfilling moment it is as if the
sweet taste of fruit of a mango a kiwi a perfect peach has been
introduced to my taste buds
When I hold you a barrier has been formed to protect all
innocents from the powerful radiance that is produced by 2
bodies who have been joined in union of mind and soul
Some say they have had, others may wish, none may possess
For how can you possess something that was formed by my
CREATOR to be enjoyed at this time
Mary may weep and Martha may moan, Noah may build and
Daniel my reveal
But with you I too can enjoy the Benevolent One's object of will

Like Dawn

I was reflecting sitting in the window trying to strike a pose like
one of my favorite jazz artists when he was playing the trumpet
looking out the window and chilling
I was reflecting sitting in the window trying to look determined
like Malcolm X. with the gun and chilling
I was sitting in the window when I realized that me being me
was cool and me being the object of her good intentions was
cooler and the coolest thing was being able to appreciate her for
herself
This lady was like the dawn; I could write some drivel about how
she was the promise after a tumultuous night
Of how she was the birth of a brand new day, of how she was
breath to a dying man, of how she was color on a tapestry of life
I could not play myself like that, so instead I related to her like
the sun and moon does to dawn
Of how dawn is the juncture, the point in the cosmos that tells
the night brother to say hello to the day sister, of the place
where these two disparate kindred souls greet, give each other
a transition report, explain their activities and merge
Of how the dawn is where if you ever doubted God existed
watch the colors, the ones that could not be present without
divine painting
Of the colors that explain everything and nothing
Watch the dawn and think of the promise of the morning
In gospel songs God rescues at dawn, in WWI movies we
attack at dawn, in sports we run at dawn, when that hour comes
we begin a new day
She represented all of this and then some, she amazed with her
style and poise, and she promised another life cycle of renewal
So I called her Dawn

Never Average

She said that she was average looking
Now I don't know Miss Lady from the Blue Bonnet white chick
but this I think deserves discussing
So I trust my internal instinct to allow these words to hit papers
and discuss the meaning average
Normal, mundane, status quo
The only thing average about this sister is the consonants and
vowels of her name, which combine to spell a special sisters
moniker

Average does not even come into focus when examining her
When checking out this sister the word that came to mind was
superlative
The thought that came to mind was how do I get to know her
The action that came to fruition was she could something
special

So when average is used to describe this sister I respectfully
disagree
The only thing average are the words on this page which
became special when I think of this sister

Perfection

"The endless pursuit of perfection" that's what an ad states
It implies that finding perfection is not attainable that it is not
feasible to achieve this goal
But they never met you

Your flaws, your shortcomings, your things that do not add up
Those are the traits that make me cherish you each day
These are the times that create memories
Those moments when it seemed desperate and it was only you
and I
Only we, only our combined faith and dedication helped us to
make it
That is perfection

Perfection means excellence, sureness, aptness, and
accomplishment
But for me it means YOU in each and every word

The most excellent way that you assure me each and every day
you acknowledge even the most trivial accomplishment in our
hectic lives is what has me falling head over heels for you again
and again and again

Every time I see you, I feel like the kid who caught his first fly
ball, scored his first touchdown, and conducted his first
successful experiment
I catch myself looking at you and remembering your slightest
nuance, your most exact tremor, and your most exquisite
moment

The summation of it all is that others may pursue perfection
But not I
Because every time I see you I know it's been found

Separation

I never called; I would have done nothing to make my presence felt
Because when it was over, it was over
She told me I was not there for her when I should have been
that I never reached out after we broke up
I replied "sister I want to tell you I was doing someone else or something else somewhere else but in actuality I was doing nothing else but thinking of you"
That every waking moment was spent in endless imaginary conversations with you
That when you said goodbye and I said hello to the possibility that you and I were no longer we but her and me, that instead of plural I was singular

I allowed myself one night to lament, one night to cry, one night to bemoan my loss
Then it was over
My man used to tell me you will never close that book if you don't recall the lessons of the words on the pages

She looked at me with big beautiful brown eyes that Willy Wonka would have envied; with a skin tone so chocolate that M & M's asked for some of her DNA

I stood and thought, with arms wrapped around her waist, head pressed to my chest, thinking of the moments we lost from each other due to pride, due to issues that in the grand scheme of things amount to nothing

And I balance those thoughts of where I have been as a man, where I have ventured on this journey called life, where I have wandered and found my way back to where we belong
Life is a mother, this woman is special and now I can sit and dig what Otis Redding was saying when he was sitting on the dock of the bay, as I try a little tenderness

There's this feeling of being upset as we allowed ourselves to forget who are we to each other, that God is the center of the universe and we were just planets in a tandem orbit
She asked me where was I when we broke up, and now I can tell her, lady I was on my journey finding the path back to us

She flows like sunlight to flowers

She flows like sunlight to flowers essential to the balance of life
She presents herself as not the wisest but the best taught after
35 moons of learning
She reflects on the years of her Pops and the virtues he
instilled, willfully thinking, righteously walking, and profoundly
impacting all she encounters
They ask names, she answers questions, and they ask for
clarity, and she provides vision
They seek harmony, and she is life calibrated equally
Specifically speaking, the sister is who she is because she
knows from where she came
Intellectually delivering, this sister walks with swagger befitting
royalty but is chastened by the basis of her origins, proud but
meager beginnings
She flows like sunlight to flowers essential as breath is to life

The Epitome of Happiness

Let me tell you my definition of happiness
See it was funny when I heard you say those words it was like
WOW, someone understands that happiness is contained within
Engendered by personal growth, personal virtues, faith and
doctrines that we personally choose
See happiness is something no one can make you, not a gift
that can be bought, not found in a companion but internalized
Is what I realized
See happiness to me is a child's smile, a basket scored, a
hearty
handshake,
Laughter after the rain, the perpetual rainbow, the icing on the
cake, the sound of unadulterated mirth,
Happiness was found at my Grandfathers funeral, at my man's
home going, at the shared memory of my first kiss, at the sound
of your voice, would be a choice
Happiness for me is when I heard your words and the lilting
tone and the fact that the Queen of Unimportant information
may have met her match
Hell, I was laughing sweating trying to think of mundane, totally
inane things that only you and I would know,
That only you and I the person who did it could know
Happiness was you telling me that you like chivalry, and me
responding and you not realizing that I was blushing like a child
See I was digging you and into your wit and style
I can't front hearing your Destiny's Child dance in your voice
was pretty different and to be specific to visualize you shaking
brought a smirk
Matter of fact I closed my eyes just to see if I could hear your
rhythm work, happiness is hearing you talk about dreams,
aspirations, force of character, strength and admission of who
you are, inquisitive, proud and pride in your family
Your recognition of a mans traits that your Dad showed you and
which you now embrace
Your faith in self, your God blessed wit and charm, Miss Thing
you are the one Top Gun
Happiness may be contained in catching a midnight flick, dinner
candlelit, a touch of palms, a fat jazz track, but last night,
closing my mental eyes I realized that hearing you
laugh and smile was the epitome of
Happiness

The steps

Check it, the sister was brown skinned, that light brown that is
café au lait or tan
Now to say she was fine is disrespect, I mean I had only known
her for a minute but she seemed like a fellow traveler, a steady
companion

Average, never that, fine, money the sister had those ruby red
lips and style that made gangsters become choir boys
The type of poise and charisma that stood out in a crowd full of
beautiful sisters
She never comes across as head strong, or full of herself, she
has not appeared out of sync with her life and her mental
environment
She works hard to be all that, she works hard to be somebody
special, she works hard to be the lady when all around are
sisters with more natural advantages but less instinctive class

How long have I known her? Mere minutes but it seems like we
been chilling for awhile
This sister is the subject of those old school jams, Rose Royce
had to be speaking of her when they sang "How can I get next
to you"
She is the reason Teddy P. broke it down for his lady

How long have I known her? Mere minutes but it seems she is
the reason brothers travel back roads in the middle of the night
to see her face for 5 minutes before work

How much do I want to know her? Why front that won't impress
the sister, why be someone I am not, that will displease this
brother, why not be the man I was raised to be, made to be
Built for speed, manufactured for longevity, promised for the
long haul

This sister stands out because of who she is, what she
represents, she is the reason why writers write stories of faithful
sisters, she is the sister made in the mold of Rebecca when
Issac saw her, she is the sister that LL Cool J rhymed about, the
one the Chi-Lites cried about, the one Etta James sang about
when she said "At last"

Urban Angel

I know who she is; she's the one that Ben E. King wanted to
stand by him
She is the one that the Jackson's wanted back, the one the
Drifters wanted to go under the boardwalk with
More importantly she is not the object of fantasy, she isn't the
subject of hyperbole, she is the one we read about in Essence
hoping to catch a glimpse as she makes not power moves but
subtle moves which have longer lasting effects
She isn't the one singing the loudest in church, she isn't the one
bragging about possessions or exclusive spots, she isn't the
one playing the front because she got tired of laying on her back
She isn't the one playing roles for which she was not bred but
she makes the bread and consumes the role
See the sister is that urban angel and she walks among us
She does not always talk the strongest
But she got that thang that ain't contained in a bottle
Can't purchase it, can't order it online, you gotta reach for her
Step to the plate and perform like the true man you are
Dig it, some sisters think making paper and acting high post is
the answer, but saying you are humble does not mean you are
humble
It means you got no humility in assigning titles to yourself
deserved or not
Peep this I see these sisters telling how they don't have a man
and they are just dating but too often dating encompasses a
meal thrown down your gullet later filled by a romp in the sack
and you want me to call you a lady
Too often dating consists of a meal at a joint rated with stars but
the only stars I know are in the heavens and if you ain't eating
at the table prepared by the Lord you can have that meal
But then here she comes, the urban angel, not in a hail of glory
but hailed as a woman, meant to be held in my arms, never held
emotionally hostage, never willfully helping to propel me on the
road to hell
A woman, she is the one that soldiers longed to return home to,
that woman that momma told you about not the one momma
warned you about, the one that makes a so-called dime feel like
a penny with a hole in it, the sister is my urban angel

Who You Be

I knew this sister who was cooler than water in the freezer; she
had the proper look, hair that was stylized but natural
Bourgeois with just a touch of class that was astonishing in a
big city
style miss lady had it all and her body revealed hips and legs
and tops and bottoms
Jeans hurt when this woman walked
I saw cats who could have been eligible bachelors for whatever
year
but when these cats tried to mack Miss Lady did not even react
Man she said everything by saying nothing, so it was something
when I the favored court clown made my move
This sister had dropped her pen and when I went to retrieve it, I
told her before I hand this over, may I ask you a question, she
smiled yes
I told her to close her physical eyes and open her mental eye
and she would view me as Adonis
That if she closed her physical eye and opened her mental eye I
am the goal of her soul yearning, I told her I will create a holy
trinity of
her past present and future
That if she looked in the past and we were not together the past
does not exist, that if she looked into the future and we were
separate the future would be as bleak and black as the dawn of
another day in hell
But at this moment in the present, I am by her side and we
coincide as one
This woman who went to A & M, spoke with excellent diction
and incredible grammar, she did not know ask me who I was,
where I was from or even who I knew, she asked me "who you
be"
In Brother Webster's dictionary the word be means to exist, to
live
And I was real, she used the term be as if she was relating to an
alien
So I told her that I be the willing and humble servant of God,
that I will be the oxygen to fill your lungs, the moisture on your
lips, the subject of the object, and the lesson for the pupil in her
eye
When the world tells her cruel and unusual things I be the
positive voice that will resonate inside her inners ear, inner ear
That I be the stimulant that will cause her heart to react, that I
be the one that will write a manuscript of love, caring and

devotion on her heart,
That I be the one that will pray to influence the elements so that her path is always lit by the power of my words
I told her "listen here miss lady", I wear glasses and contacts but I am not superman, I cannot leap tall buildings, I cannot move mountains but I be the one that will ask our Lord to make a way through mountainous obstacles that may stand in our path
That I am a poet, emphasis on being poor, meaning I have no money, but that I am rich beyond belief because I have the pleasure and treasure of knowing you
Listen, I was digging the sister but I did not want to gas her up too much, so I didn't tell her that Foot Locker had sent me a text message saying she had so much soul they wanted to franchise her, that Sealy Posturpedic said she had so much poise and backbone they wanted to patent her, that one day I was out running and the Kool-Aid man ran me down and said she had so much flavor they wanted to market a campaign based solely on her name, that if I ever say something to cause fear, anger, or apathy to cross her face, I would be like Daniel in the old Testament and open up the windows of my soul three times a day asking my God to allow my Grandmothers to commune with me via my dreams whenever I needed counsel regarding decisions that I make which could impact our lives together
Y'all should have seen her the sister had a walk that was a killer but a smile that was a life giver
She had the class of Nancy Wilson and the style of Lady Day
I told her that to talk to her at that moment I am forced to use modern day slang, chop and lace it with ancient text from a long forgotten language using her mind like a blank wall and write a hieroglyphic of love that only she and I could decipher, so she grabbed my hand and we walked away talking without words

URBAN

Urban Intro

This is called the Urban section because when it is all said and done I am a child of the city, 111th street, the Wild Hundreds. Both of my parental units came from the same blocks, and ultimately this urban up-bringing is trapped in my innards, courses throughout my veins. It does not define me but the sound of the big city is what helps to fuel my writings. Traveling downtown, on the El, the Hoagy Shop, seeing hustlers, and politicians, doctors and lawyers all come back to the block, forgetting their present stations in life but remembering Morgan Park. Remembering Chicago, remembering the real Taste of Chicago, ChicagoFest, the Rink, The Loop, playing ball, Hip-Hop in the park, block parties, gang banging friends, watching the way we wear our hats, where we partied.

2 Friends and a Love Child

"You stupid person, you need to check my track record" so said the vocal Harlem maven "Exactly what are your standards of greatness? Because you say things that are barely good are great"
So as I scream to have myself heard both internally and at the world I realize I am blessed
For some people have running buddies and some have muse's but me I have both my conscience and intellect craving satisfied by 2 who stroll down paths who respect me enough to criticize me, see it's inexplicable that that because of their involvement my writing is no longer typical, as I strive to reach ever increasing pinnacles
Of thought and sound so my words resound and bounce back
Like sounds that react for bats like intellectual radar
Informing me when my quarry or goals are near and within reach
Providing therapy through speech
2 friends and a love child enjoying life as we careen through the galaxy on this mud-ball held in place by a thought called gravity
Verbally stepping on stars using the tails of comets as jump rope as we double-dutch with angels, play 2 squares with denizens of universes that usually bemoan the sight of our existence
Resistance is futile but for 2 friends and a Love child the brutal concept of living is tempered by life's rhythm with their wisdom
We bound galaxies and see wonders in words, playing bid whist in Valhalla, BINGO on Olympus, for yesterday we chased unworthy supplicants to the art with angry African gods as our guides, as we 3 band of scribes of the spoken word vibe, point souldiers of the Neo- Soul tribe
Traveling back roads and byways. Making U-Turns in life both physically and mentally
Have you ever watched master chefs cook and breaks eggs well we break pens as we invite others to fulfill their knowledge and linguistic appetite as their mental's bend to the ways and means of our trip through the spoken word scene
2 friends and a love child have scaled heights that tower above the Alleghenies Pike's Peak combined with the Sears Tower
With them I have increased my power as Fuzzyhead and I constructed "In me I
see her" in about half of the hour
But still I digress I am the love child rolling with 2 Friends

12 blocks in Roseland

Within 1 block of traveling through the concrete
jungle that I call home I pass one black man who has
been downtrodden by a society in which he fought to
keep it free
Passing one black man who finds solace in a bottle
that promises respite from a world where he defended a
way of society that does not defend him

Within 2 blocks I pass this man and 2 young girls who are on
divergent paths but yet they don't know it as they
strive to keep up with the images kicked out on 106
and Park as they feel dueling pangs of wanting to be
young girls and at the same time live the lives of the
images of the cheap non-talented singing women that
the media calls a diva choosing between mini-skirts
and wanting to play in the park but they are told that
it is their body and they can give it any man who they
please especially if he has rims

Within 3 blocks I pass these 2 little girls, the drunk
vet and 3 liquor stores owned by men who saw our
shores as lands of opportunity but who learned that
they were shunted and given opportunity like the
cowboys and settlers of old who conquered the native
man
Except the native they conquer now is dark pigmented
and they are convinced he wants black and milds, and
40 ounces, and loose cigarettes, and they like to sell
knock-off gas at exorbitant rates while looking to
date our young women while they sell our families meat
way past the expiration date, conscripted to a fate
but still we don't hate

Within 4 blocks of the drunken vet, the 2 lost little
girls and the 3 overpriced local stores I passed 4
storefront churches that swore that there charismatic
speakers/preachers spoke the word and could bring the truth as
they contributed to a never fulfilling building fund,
then I question myself am I the one to really question
their purpose or am I the one who is lacking vision
and cannot get with these righteous people on a
mission?

After the 5 blocks in which I passed the drunken vet,

the 2 lost little girls and the 3 overpriced local
stores and the 4 storefront churches I pass a mosque
and 5 Muslim brothers, 1 from the Nation, 2 Sunni, 2
Shiite with a vision of tomorrow and who to fight,
from them I learned to view the world from a
non-western eye and fly in the face of convention and
take freedom from a universe that the networks only
mention as terrorists and they taught me to peacefully
resist and still be a righteous Christian

Reflecting as I get to Block 6 and it's shining internally

So I continue on to Block 7 and parley with 7 cool cats from
around the way, saying "Yo K. what's the steez of the
day", I reply I can't call it, and no motion is slow
motion, as I notice my man hiding the rocks in his
hands, they punch the clock like drug dealers had a
union and my man was the shop steward and he had to
make sure that the union members were on the assembly
line for the consumers called drug addicts as I
bounded through traffic to the other side to vibe

On block 8 I see 8 people with whom I had broke bread and
gave
some dap, see two of my girls were into women and two
of my guys were into other guys, one chick was cool and
she walked on both sides of the street and the 3
others blended into the background waiting to get
chose I suppose

9 blocks down and I have passed 9 houses of the
elderly who have seen better days and remember black
folks had pride and standing in community living glory
days that in comparison to now is so embarrassing, not
realizing that we are the offshoot of their offspring
who turned Malcolm's vision into a sight blended with
King's dream

10 blocks traversed and I have trudged through sights
that to an outsider would be incongruous in their view
never questioning our existence taking in all sights
and sounds while some see urban decay I see a
community of pride and of ones hanging on, passing by
corners where we were banging on garbage cans giving
each other props filling in the gaps of the mind mixed

in with sounds of buses as we rush to corporate
plantations we call jobs

11 blocks and I count the previous encounters and how
I remember the 11 people I lost before I knew it, like
Jamal Pippen, Ellen Williams, and Alex Rosalio, Malik
James, Lemuel Holmes, and Ryan Green, Jason Tillman,
Blanche and Golden Tillman, Stanford and Lemuel
Now there are 3 names that are linked because of the worst
way they were buried or died on my birthday and count them 11
names
etched into my heart all walked my streets and we all talked,
all branded me with their lessons

12 blocks down on a particular side of town that
astounds some in the complex simplicity of growing up
in the inner city, we got busy on those corners and
lives were lost on that one, catching shorties in the
alleyways smoking and rolling a fat one, seeing the
cops and the thugs only separated by colors and a
badge, I have life of memories lived in these 12
blocks, a casual outsider did not see the richness in
my world and said this ain't the way it should, or
talked about what could, I replied its all good its
just 12 blocks on a day in the hood

Freedom is a Bitch

Freedom is the worst whore ever known to man
Freedom is like a woman who allows you to have her way with
her and when you get used to the ready steady throb, the throes
of ecstasy that this harlot, this woman of the scarlet letter F gets
you used to
Then the bitch ups and leaves
Freedom is the type of hoe who will get down with those who
have the biggest funds and
If not them then the ones with the biggest guns
Freedom spreads her legs for anyone who can afford her
services
Freedom is disguised by many false guises and has many
different purposes
Freedom is at the same time pimped and pimps, for look at
some of the whores Freedom has on her stroll
Freedom has a trick called Equality and a two-faced whore
named Liberty, but the worst of one of them all is Indivisible
Justice for all
Freedom causes men to jump overboard and be devoured just
to say that they died free
Freedom caused women to sacrifice themselves and their seed
just to say that they died free
Freedom caused a horror called the Diaspora
Freedom caused Brother Malcolm to tell the world he would be
free "By any means Necessary"
Freedom caused Brother Martin to "tell us that he knew he
would not get to the Mountaintop with us"
Freedom caused Brother Medgar Evers to be tantalized and
tempted by this wench and as he stepped towards his home he
was killed but he died Free
But friends I come to tell you that the bitch has been caught,
albeit fleetingly but she has been caught
For when Brother Jimi played that guitar, playing that National
Anthem he captured her in those notes
When Brother Stevie sings of a "Higher Ground" he captures
her in those notes
When Sister Billy Holliday told us about "Strange Fruit" Lord
grant us the serenity of her testimony she captured her in those
notes
Freedom made us get tear gassed, made us endure our women
being bitten by dogs
Makes us pay our money into coffers so Freedom can be
delivered to others
My Muslim brothers and sisters try to attain Freedom through

Jihad's
My Christian brothers and sisters try to attain freedom through
ministries
When you see a kid on the playground with a mile wide smile
playing
basketball he is
Free
When I hear a country boy singing of his home he is Free
For Freedom knows that we are junkies fiending for her fix so
that we can say we are free
Freedom

Good mourning

As I thought of the eulogy that would be delivered I pondered
the difference between a sad home going and the words
celebrating a good mourning
I thought of his Momma as she celebrated the arrival of my
friend, if she pondered the destructive forces that predicted the
annihilation of her male child
As a child she spoke to us of the politics of life in the U.S. of A,
in Chicago as a male black child, she tried to prepare us for the
temptations, for the residual effects of racism, as she embodied
the tenacity of a modern Harriett in this sophisticated seemingly
wretched existence called life
Her words were sustenance verbal manna to modern black
Jews in this Babylon called America
As she tutored us so the world would not make us intellectually
ignorant, time after time, she taught us that life was to be
treated with reverence
That daily prayers were more than ritualistic affirmations; I wish
she spoke with a Tourette's syndrome of reality as society
dictated it
That her sacrifices were not in vain

That the omnipotent faith she possessed was not rendered
oblivious in the face of modern adversity
The sustenance of our existence was the idealized romance we
shared called fun
We attempted to re-establish good old days that seemingly
never existed
We were smartly stupid, almost catatonic in our exuberance as
we celebrated a life of joy, damn amazing as I stood at the dais
and mentally waxed nostalgic about where we had been and
where we were going
Time no longer mattered, as I recalled the sounds of LL Cool J
blasting down the street, fighting the power with Public Enemy,
of Rakim belling "I ain't no joke", the attitude that we could
acquire the altitude to be ....free,
that I and he and us would not wallow in the swamps of
ineptitude and city life
That we would not succumb to the abhorrent forces of society
that should not have been loosed on the worst sinner in any of
Dante's levels of hell
Yes they should have told us but No they refused
I wish they had told me that she could only love my friend as a
Momma and me as a mentor I wish that she had told me that on

the day of my friends home going I would be called upon to give him a good mourning

A good mourning they ask as I recall my friend

A good mourning they call it as my words flow like water over a rock of futility as I want my friend to rise like Black Jesus commanded Lazarus

I cried and realized that my memories would provide me with a good mourning

III Sounds

As the sounds of Whodini's friends wafted through in the background we sat on stone steps feeling the freedom of urban living

We slapped five and played the dozens, we ran to parks and played ball under the lights, we ran near the tracks and watched the trains roar off over the horizon, always wondering where it was heading, promising one day that we would follow, because from our point of view we saw the Sears Tower way off in the distance, like a promise, a beacon that beckoned us

We went from Granny's to down the street to up the street to Ms. Odessa's corner store for a pickle with a peppermint in the middle with hot sauce on it for good effect and when
We got sick and went to Dr. Pedro's for some soul medicine and good advice,
We went to Sunday school and we praised God, and we had a picture of a black Jesus that was 10 feet high on the back wall looking down on us and smiling
Now down home folks went to Mt. Calvary and those who been here a minute went to Beth Eden and upright people went to Arnett and the Pope's guys to Holy Name of Mary and when it was time to go home to the Universal God they were all prepared by the Williams Chapel

We chased the cat and knew that all cats were not feline but some cats walked on two legs and talked hip and spoke with emotion while at the same displaying their coolness, they spoke with bravado and talked of how the only thing they feared was running out of time to conquer the world
We knew the stick up kids, and saw the Vets from Vietnam who seemingly longed to walk in the shadows as if they were afraid for the world to see them in the light of the war that they fought on two fronts
We went to rallies by the anti-establishment parties, parleyed with Muslims, and talked with the remnants of the Black Panthers; spoke with reverence of Mark Clark and Fred Hampton
Saw police brutality and how they would arrest Momma's and sisters and Fathers and brothers for pleading with them not to beat the suspect because all suspects have families

And how we saw police calm Momma's and sisters and Fathers and brothers when they delivered the news that so and so was killed, because all victims have families
We saw older junkies lecture to younger junkies not to follow their junkie path but yet and still they walked alongside them silently praying that they could beat their Jones, which they would not need to rob to get that bump in the night, that they would not do things no human should do to satisfy their craving
We saw older whores who were now reformed and who lamented and gnashed their teeth in an effort to run from their past as their shapely daughters silently pondered their future
We knew cats who rode the 5 and those who rode the 6, we were told stories of King David, and Hoover, and Vice-lord Prince's, and older chicks that carried their man's blade or gat
We saw empty bottles get cleaned up by civic-minded people, and walked to the mall trying to avoid racism of the worst sort
The type of racism that encouraged you to buy and shop but when shopping was done you changed from a consumer to a loiterer
We walked steps in endless processions and hit el stops with the Defender in one hand and the other clutching the big kids hand as we made our way down to the Museum, and were treated to new wonders in Science and Industry and stories of DuSable
We watched Russ Ewing negotiate the surrender of another brother on the run
We watched Fahey Flynn and my man John with the applejack hat
We saw A.M. Chicago become the footstep for Harpo productions
We lived and died on 111th street, we marched and stood on 111th street, we saw life on 111th street, we left 111th street for Kankakee, we left 111th street for downtown, we called it the concrete Nile, we called it the cradle to the grave, we saw it give life and take it away
We learned life, love, saw pimps become players who became respected who became L-7's, I saw meek guys go to college and come back as Nupe's and Q's and A Phi A, I saw generations nurtured on the soul food that was not healthy and saw this food sustain us all
We got beat, and won, and lost all in the same afternoon, we created and imitated and proclaimed and in the same breath lamented reality
We could relate to Cornbread, Earl and me because the hood all over the world is full of Cornbread's, Earl's and us

We knew cats that could beat Jimmy Connors but white folks
already had Arthur Ashe
We played baseball and saw the cats with souped up rides
head to Doty Road with pinks and come back as a passenger
but smiling
We listened to older cats talk about fighting and gang banging
with cats from the Wild West Side and how exotic North Side
black folks were, and how the ones over East were slick and
fast, and thug cats who went downtown and snatched
pocketbooks and picked up chicks from the bus station on
Randolph and the working stiffs who lived out dreams in clubs
on the weekend blowing paychecks and the rent or mortgage
just to be the man for an evening

Listen the story of my hood is universal, it's within me, and
within us, from spitting the illest in H-Town, to rockin in Dallas,
to finding my other home in Austin, L.A. got stories, NYC got
people, Detroit got it's own thing, but Chi-Town got the ill
sounds of the 1 double L, 111th Ill Street

Nothing but two turntables, some mikes and speakers

Nothing but two turntables, some mikes and speakers
No one told me that on 10/30/2002, on that date they were
going to take part of my soul with them
No one told me that on that day, part of me was going to be
forcefully ripped from my soul
No one told me that on that day thoughts of my family and
friends, memories that I had collected would be gone, stolen
and I did not even know the thief
See on that day one of the cornerstones of my childhood was
gone; one of the pleasantries of remembering of being with my
Grandmother and Grandfather was stolen from me
One semester in high school I did real good and my
Grandparents gave me $5.00 and I ran to the record store and
bought this 12 inch record and this tape and boy y'all should
have seen this bow-legged inner city wild child who was a B-
Boy, be enjoyed by voices of a society that was being destroyed
by its own forces
I had made my choice and soon in the basement you could hear
the voice of Peter Piper picked peppers and Run rocked
rhymes
And my Grandmother and Grandfather were upstairs and they
just laughed while outside gangs banged guns and wiped out
each others dreams
But inside that basement I drowned out the noise of the hood
with these 3 Kings from Queens, I remember going with my
cousin and he and his crew of roughneck guys and we would
bum rush the door and we would scatter and they would find me
a seat down front and then would take my ticket and scalp it,
But they stopped when those cats from a whole different city
took the stage
When one of these apostles came out and took off his shoe and
we felt like an army and in unison whether we had or Nikes or
Reeboks or Kmart specials, we all shouted out "My Adidas"
But on 10/30/02 part of those memories were taken from me
Man I used to ride the subway late night and watch cats getting
mugged and I had fights at home with my Pops and a cat was
trying to keep his head on right and one thing that I relied on
was these cats music
Of how I used to cry to God while they comforted me out of my
headphones, of how my internal scream was soothed and
turned into an eternal dream when they talked about the master
of a disco scratch
Man we would put out the plastic mat and the local dope boys
would have dookie rope chains and belt buckles with names on

them and lees and four finger rings and have these fly women with the salt and pepper hairstyles just looking crazy mad hard while these cats from Queens told us about hard times
Have you ever seen the biggest darkest cat in the world who had a head so big that his bowler like Run's was too small but you could not tell him that he was not cool as these Kings from Queens
Man I used to practice in the basement and pray that if Run or D had an issue with each other I would be prepared to step in and take either one's place but I knew I could never take the place of one member of the crew
And that cat was taken from us on 10/30/02
On that day we lost what I consider the Duke Ellington of the turntable, I lost the man who provided the music that soothed the ignorance inside of me
See when I was a young ugly nerd people could ride me all day about my physical nature, read all day about my lisp, about my gear but they could not get with me about a few things, sports, talking garbage and Hip-Hop more importantly rapping
Man when I would do a talent show I would get hype backstage by listening to Run DMC, I would imitate the scratches of Jam Master Jay over and over again
Me and Mark would come out on stage and do our thing and even the cats who hated me, even the many young ladies who turned me down for a date had to shut up and listen
When I grabbed that mike, I was Run, I was D, I was J, I was cool
I used to hear the young ladies say "K may be ugly but that sucker sure can rhyme"
When I was in a battle I imagined that I had to audition for my favorite B-Boy crew in the world and this was my one shot at glory
The reason I like to believe that I never made the Olympics is because one day in the spring I cut track practice to go see this joint called Krush Groove
In my heart I believe that I could have run a 10 flat with that one extra practice but I chose to go to see my guys throw down in this movie
As a result Carl Lewis was spared a whipping he did not even know he had coming because the 3 Kings from Queens were on the screen and I was there on an unseasonably warm spring evening in a nylon running suit looking hot as a tamale in a microwave but I was cool
But these memories were taken away on 10/30/02
On that day somebody who looks like one of us stomped and smashed my memories

Smashed the images I had of my Grandparents, smashed the images of my cousin, smashed the comfortable sounds that I had in my head that consoled me when the world dealt me a cruel blow

On 10/30/02 part of me ceased to exist and on that day part of me ceased to live

On that day someone chose to wantonly take a building block of my culture and destroy it

If they had asked me I would have told them that a little big nosed, bad eyesight bow legged cat would have pleaded with them

Would have told them of how this guy represented dreams, of how this man who I never met provided a mental sanctuary that his music was like the song of a true minstrel

That this man that he so wantonly shot and killed snuffed out the dreams of countless kids who wanted nothing more

Oh God the beauty of his music was purity; it contained a raw essence that was innocent in form, practice and performance, he took what we did in the park and showed the world that we did not need bands that we did not need high-tech nothing but two turntables, some mikes and speakers

Peace & Blessings

Peace and Blessings is what the man stated to his opposite
I mean they were like arguing in the most violent manner
possible
Using terms such as complete annihilation and blasphemy
And depicting their opposite speaker as being ignorant and
stupid
I walked up on this scene on a street corner watching one
speaker mesmerize the crowd
And the opposite speaker enchant his audience
One painted a picture of perfection and told of the path one
must take
Another painted a picture of how you need faith and works to
receive your just reward

One talked of slave mentalities, the other of a mentality of the
blame game
You guys should have seen it, should have heard these
profound speakers
These obvious learned scholars, these heralds of the truth
I stood and gravitated like a horse to water, drinking deeply from
the bottomless well of facts and innuendo and profound
statements
My thirst for knowledge was being quenched beyond belief by
these two wellsprings of life's lessons
They would yell back and forth from street corner to street
corner using their intellect like a weapon, dueling like Earl Flynn
in Robin Hood, I could imagine hearing their powerful
statements clashing like two swords, almost like a Bip Bap pow
from 1960's Batman
Oh man, you guys should have seen it, these verbal jousters of
unimagined proportions, breaking it down how the man was
holding us down, leaving us without any doubt about who was
telling the TRUTH
Then I stopped and I thought how more people have died telling
the truth than anything else in the world, and I contemplated
how these men, these weekly speakers were fighting with words
over GOD
The passion they exhibited in educating us, one telling us that
we are deaf dumb and blind to the ways of mankind, and the
other saying how God will not lead his sheep astray, both
illuminating the others arguments with parallel parables
Then I stopped and I thought how these two men were acting
like sworn enemies, using scare tactics and justifying them, you

would have thought that J. Edgar Hoover had heard these guys had pictures of him in drag the way they were carrying on, and I realized the profound truth of how more people have died in the name of God than anything else

That there words and actions and suggestions would not shake my faith but inspire me to find my own way

So at that moment on that cool fall Saturday during my high school years, I turned up the headphones on my Walkman, plugged in Rakim, pumped up the volume and walked away secure in the knowledge that I may never find the Truth but I would find my own path to God

So many of Today

So many of today's revolutionaries are so willing to say what they will die for
But how many are willing to tell you what they are willing to live for, to stick around and suffer through the change that they so eloquently tell us must come

They paint the picture that it is so noble to come before you and yell that they would gladly place their physical lives on the line, and while that it is cool, what if they were forced to stand around and look at the world they created

Patrick Henry said give me liberty or give me death but what if he was forced to look at a society which he helped foster in which the indigenous people, the ones we so conveniently brand as native American, showed him that they were not equal and they needed liberty

Or the black folks which they said were ¾ of a person wanted liberty
Or the poor white farmers who did not have access to the system were denied certain liberties
Or women who were treated as afterthoughts

They make us believe that they will automatically go into a glory filled heaven because they gave up their lives for their cause

But what if God in all of the Creator's wisdom said no, you gave up the flesh and blood but you did not change one mind
That you spent so much time running around trying to get killed in the name of a cause that you forgot how to live

I mean we have deluded entire generations into believing that dying for a cause, which may not be that noble, is worth your life
This cuts across racial barriers because realistically how much difference is there between James Dean, TuPac Shakur, Kurt Cobain, and BIGGIE Smalls, all lived fast, lived hard, and died young and we celebrate them
From Rebel without a cause, to Teen Spirit, to Pour out a little Liquor, to Mo Money Mo Problems

We tell women about the noble Joan of Arc, we tell Muslim kids about a heroes heaven, we tell Asian kids about kamikazes but what we don't tell them is that it's harder to stand and live through the change they want to bring about

Funny thing how people always are quick to tell black kids that at the start of the Revolutionary War Crispus Attucks died but not the ideal he was trying to live for

The world knows all about Gandhi and how he was assassinated, and King and X. but how many know the story of Martin Luther, how he brought change and lived to a ripe old age

The next time you see one of these revolutionaries with their red black and green armbands, hats cocked backwards, stylistic talk, rhetoric ask them if they are willing to expend the same energy in being a living martyr as they are in sticking around and helping to change

The Kitchen Table

I remember sitting at my Grandmothers Kitchen table
and how she and my Grandfather taught lessons that
resonate deep within our souls uniting all of us who
came in contact with them in an unbreakable chain
Almost like druids of the hood
I recall that my Grandmother taught us to never bring
plastic or paper plates to your table because you try
to bring quality into your home
And plastic and paper plates like so many other things and even
some people
we may dress them up but they are still transient and cheap
I recall of how my Grandfather would drink coffee so
black and so strong that even when cream was added to
the mixture the cream became one with the black
To this day I try to avoid the cream in my coffee
Because while the cream can add something extra its
nothing like jet-black java
See now our childhood was not idyllic in the sense
that we had a lot or lived in a fancy mansion, I mean
it was the sho'nuff hood
The same hood where you could not walk in the park
after dark because cats got shot
Where a 10-year-old boy killed a twelve-year-old girl
and it made the cover of National magazines
But in my mentals I still picture the scene
Of Sunday morning Sunday school and after Sunday
school head to Martha's or another local eatery and parley
with the Muslim cats and listen as they talk about the white
man's religion while they sell suits and bean pies out of the
trunks of there
cars, but to outsiders they were hustlers but to us they were
like local stars
I remember when you could get counsel from a priest
back before they were trying to get a piece of
someone's kid
Before the stylish thing was selling dope and bragging
about doing a bid
I remember a neighborhood where NBA stars came from and
played and walked the asphalt and represented for us,
before they became insulated from the places that
produced them
Where they get swallowed in a world that uses them and
we watch on the boob tube as we lose them
I was taught that a Post Man and a teacher were true

43

revolutionaries who made it possible for us to sit in
coffee spots and plot the revolution
Of how every Saturday morning was like a parade
because everyone knew someone walking down the street
and I never did meet a stranger
I mean if someone got done it wasn't random, when cats
had beef they held court in the streets
Of how at the Roseland Theater pimps had their women
and always told us young cats to achieve to be
something else
Before the dawn of the age of the "Pimp/Rappers"
See sitting at that kitchen table on 111th street on
the Southside of Chicago I was provided a plethora of
answers to issues I did not even know I would
encounter
I learned to believe in God and what belief stood for,
I learned that you protect your family and your
friends, I learned first hand how cops are cops to us
but police men to other folks
I heard the philosophy of Dr. Richard Pryor who helped
us escape when we used to sneak in the basement and
listen to his dirty jokes
We had Fat Albert Saturdays and Charlie Brown specials and
how my grandmother taught us that if you don't have
it, you don't need it but what you receive you protect
it and respect it
Of my Grandfathers philosophy of Quality over Quantity
and what it was like to be the child of two local
legends my Moms and my Pops
And how even in the midst of strife love never stops
Childhood friends who used to play army with and shoot
each other and run like we were on a track now shoot
narcotics and have track marks on their arms and
between their toes
I suppose, in the kitchen it wasn't just a place to satiate
your hunger
I wish more of us had kitchen tables when we were
younger

Urban Preachers

My theology is recorded on pavement with words written in
blood, scriptures formed by everyday deeds
The high priests of our urban religion can be found sitting in
corners of barbershops, or porches, with verses etched into
their faces testaments contained on their bloodstained hands
Playing checkers or dominoes moving pieces on boards as
incestuous imperial monarchs moved armies in efforts to
colonize and enslave free people the world over
The only pyramids that they see are downtown skyscrapers
Our river Nile is miles of subway and elevated train tracks
Hieroglyphics are billboards scrawled with graffiti
Buses are slave wagons transporting these modern day slaves
not to fields of wheat but to corporate plantations
The overseer over stands over the land that is overran with
those who truly cannot distinguish between acquiring goals and
furthering the modern day slavery plot
Some smoke narcotics thinking they are escaping from the
system but what they smoke is not illegal it's just another of the
man's products
In the antebellum south, cotton was planted but some farmers
hated the crop because it was harsh and destroyed the soil
through constant use
In modern America/Babylon they keep the people confused by
planting the same seeds of empty victory, countless slogans,
charges of treason because the current slaves question struggle
without a purpose
We watch and listen to educated minstrels who find more
solace and waste more space speaking of hard times and
adversity, which they have never experienced
Sometimes we listen to poets who create fictionalized ghettoes
in pieces they designed while the listen slash voter is treated as
point on a rating system
The leader achieves his points by ostracizing the world; the poet
achieves their point by constructing slums and constructing
endless prose of maladies of degradation, of fantasy, as they
would have us believe that they suffer like the real life slaves of
the Civil War era
Both extremes serve one purpose an obsession with justifying
their existence
Now some will say that I am ignorant because I refuse to
believe in their false fights for freedom and others will say
brother be quiet because you will piss off one of those freedom
poets and start a fight

And I will reply like Frederick Douglass
*"Those who profess to favor freedom, and yet deprecate
agitation, are men who want crops without plowing up the
ground. They want rain without thunder and lightning"*
So I sit in coffee spots and these hip poetry places and if I
closed my eyes and believed all I heard, according to these
artists we live in an era where every other black woman is
Harriet Tubman, and every other Black man is Nat Turner
But in all likelihood every one or other poet is more akin to Step
and Fetch it
The only jungle I have ever walked in is urban, the only herd I
have ever migrated in, was during rush hour traffic, the only
jungle rhythms I danced to were break beats but it does not
mean I neglect, abuse or forget our history, it just means I
neglect abuse and try to forget these poets and their whack
story

Urban Stimuli

It's 1986 and there is Eddie Bauer, McDonald's, Kroch and Brentano's, the A Train to the 9-5
Fall Saturdays in the city that gave the world Cooley High, Florida and James Evans
She and I headphones plugged in opposite sides of the train, heading downtown playing it cool
We glance at each other, then we look at each other and we play it cool
The young sister got flavor, Swatch watch, leather jacket, Guess jeans and all
We hit the street at the same time when we stop at the corner nervously smile and began to chat and play it cool
Now normally no issue because Miss Lady is fly, cute and with style
Except for one thing, SHE'S A WHITE GIRL
You see this cutie pie that caught my eye that rode on the El as I, the same one with the nice physique, style and flavor was not of my color, not of my race but we played it cool
We chatted, liked the same things, listened to the same music, responded to the same urban stimuli
The same urban stimuli that caused me to stop, that caused me to pause before I make that move
That famed urban stimuli, which caused me to react as if it was original sin for me to want her and her to want me, which would not be cool
The same signs were being sent; the same things were being thought the same emotive actions were being made
She knew the latest dances, hit the fly spots, had all the lingo and it was natural
She even smoked an La, gave props to Mother Africa, had the best intentions in her speech, tones of urban America, she walked with a swagger, and sure of herself she was playing it cool
We reached for the salt shaker at the same time, hands brushed, eyes locked, and emotions were evident I wanted to reach, I wanted to hold, I wanted to go body to body, she wiggled her finger and I got close, a kiss ensued and we looked around and people were either looking or not looking but it FELT LIKE THE WHOLE WORLD WAS WATCHING US
Here I am the kid from one eleven ill street, the angry black teenager, the quintessential Neo-soldier before the term was even coined and I am looking into the prettiest green eyed girl I have ever met, and I am not thinking about the injustices that

her obvious European ancestors committed, I am not thinking
about Apartheid and how Nelson Mandela was incarcerated, I
am thinking like a 15 year old, cocky city kid, who is excited
because this fly girl is digging me
Thoughts of letting down the race are not crossing my mind,
being called a sell-out is not the topic, but yet and still those
titles are hanging over me like a social death sentence, like a
flying guillotine blade of societal proportions ready to decapitate
me
Ready to pull my hole card, it's as if my Great Uncles who ran
from the south due to racism are staring at me from on high and
shaking their heads
We stopped, held hands, walked into the cool fall Saturday
breeze and snuggled, we went to Grant Park and
communicated, we exchanged numbers knowing that the others
phone number would never be dialed, we enjoyed that time,
those stolen moments
Those moments when she and I played it cool

Verses in Inner City Scriptures and Essays from Concrete Sandlots

We used to play red light green light, and then it seemed Simon said grown up time
Put away the toys mature young girls became local chicks some grew up and adopted the guise of the older ladies

I knew one feminine sister who is now more man than most men, but when we were younger, she had on pretty dresses and frilly tops, the apple of the eye, center of the core
She was who she was but not anymore

Cats from the Boy Scouts or Webelos acted like we were way below instead of selling magazine subscriptions they started moving blow, so like yo
Go back to the core concrete sandlots, playing basketball, fast as all, while the gang bangers spray painted on the walls

My man from five years old, 1st, 2nd grade, 3rd grade, 4, we made it through 5th but in sixth I left the mix
North side here I come, Wrigley field, from the White Sox to the Cubbies, I saw sailors from the Great Lakes have $25.00 reasons for the late date, youngsters smoking, old cats yelling, rebelling in the whole world, I celebrate the time with my old girl
But she's a new one dig the ways I do one; pursue the money like a Keebler Elf

Styles versatile like black label top shelf
What's my name, can't forget it, I take memories of the block and went down South and now I spit it
Critics on the gonads, go rad, I got a college degree and a whole lot of debt, after school pledged Phi NU Pi and learned how to step

Protect my locale, hanging with my old crew called my old pals El Hajj Malik El Shabazz, MLK, leading peaceful marches, holding hands, chunks of concrete are like grains of sands
Forget the man of the hour, decades are in a blur, lifetimes for my friend 87 years, which is years in seconds doled out by the man in black because he said my man sold cracks, but mis facts are mis-stated and now my man is missed

My eyes are getting misty cause I miss her, my eyes are getting watery because I miss her
Small town girl, big city cat, match made on fiber optics dig the ways we rock it
I am who I am, and what I am, is the son of Sylest, prodigy of Bill, so step to the plate
Verses in Inner Scripture and Essays from Concrete Sandlots

When we betrayed Hip-Hop

And Ezra Boggs said he would write it but the Pepsi generation
would probably just re-mix it and sell the boot-leg copies
And so it began it went from the rhythmic clap, claps, to odes of
rivals getting clapped over lyrics
It went from graf writers, aerosol artists representing crews and
styles to cats representing factions of drug lords
It went from shell toes, and mock necks turntables with pennies
on the arm, scratch pads and copters
To coppers forming units because rappers and breakers, and
writers, and dj's became menaces to society and I don't mean
the movie
The culture spread from NY to LA and to the W-I-N-D-Y C-I-T-Y
only to be betrayed by those who replaced the sound of
sneakers running to the floor to break to the sounds of sneaker
type cats who would rather break the rules and yell Hip-Hop
My culture was never built on foundations of innocence and
charm, my culture never got where it is because they played fair
and the powers that be allowed us to participate
Out of street violence, out of a need for something better, the
culture was borne, but out of a desire to quell the roar of guns,
now we are moving to quell the roar of greed, out of the storm of
the streets we have elevated an art form of lyrical innovation by
Uncle, Rakim, Kris, T, and others to the art form of who can
provide the best eulogy which is usually followed by a desire to
stop the violence but wait we started that back in 1988
Hip-Hop isn't dead, but when you got cats going from pro-black
to always explaining as to why they dealt crack, to bragging on
records about deeds real or not, that the goals of mic control are
incongruous to their goals of the next Benz, the next opportunity
to make a good girls knees bend, that the only ghetto's are not
physical structures but mental environments
Hip-Hop isn't dead, when we replaced cries of my Adidas to
cries of who shot so and so, and b better have my money, to
yells of that's just my Baby's daddy, to inciting lyrics of the
better the crime the more propulsion there is
Hip-Hop isn't dead, question if half of these cats who strive to
keep it real, kept it real, and told younger cats that if you get
caught smoking dope you won't have a high powered
mouthpiece but a public defender and you will probably cop a
plea I wonder if they would listen
If in efforts to keep it real when these cats in Hip-Hop get busted
why don't they face the charges like women and men they say
they are and take it like a G

The G's I know, lectured to the young brothers and sisters to achieve on other levels
Ignorance masquerading as my art form, magazines yelling about how commercial Hip-Hop is as they lure youngsters from limited means with images of flash and dash
Hip-Hop isn't dead we betrayed it
And Ezra Boggs said he would write it but the Pepsi generation would just re-mix it and sell the boot-leg copies

Where I rest

On the way from home to where I Rest
As I rode through the air returning to the place I rest, I was stunned
You see I had met this southern lady who had a vibe that was appealing
That was startling, that even caused a cool cat from the city of big shoulders to pause, to think
I had been hustling with my friends enjoying my home but there was this smile which crept to my face whenever I thought of her
My guys were telling me about their ladies, their wives, their special friends and I just kept smiling
Her style and wit was something to behold
After much smiling and smirking this name was told
I said to my man that she was witty, that she was into research and development
And I wanted to research and develop how to be with her
You see Larenz Tate and Nia Long gave the world a glimpse of my city
But I longed to invite her to my home to hold her hand
While walking down Michigan Avenue to eat at outdoor cafe's
To bump and grind to a reggae rhythm and rhyme
To feed her some of the delicacies that pleases me
to show her where I was raised
to show her where I praised God
Where I made my mark as a man
Where I had fights both won and lost
Where my soul was forged, where I cried, the streets I walked the places I bled
All I want to do is hold her hand
To kiss her in the twilight of a Windy city night
To take her down my tree-lined streets
To eat at a late night joint
In a crowd of beautiful sisters I see only her
In an auditorium of wonderful sounds I only hear her
I can tell her that I ain't perfect
That I get nervous, I get flustered, I need to be held, I am not all I can be
But I am a man
To tell her I will not play her or me but I think of we
In a Windy City view in a city rivaled by few in the world, in a place where Nubian sisters who speak my dialect understand my slang

I think of a southern woman who is sexier than them all, more attractive than any because she is herself
As I ride this plane back to the place I rest back to where I am existing, I look out the window at the stars and imagine that they are pointing my way to her
See this is where a young cat would play himself an say I need you, I want you, I love you
But as a man I realize when a lady approaches
Being real is what I have researched and developed all these years just to reach now
Her southern charms are turned on by Northern style in an effort to hear her smile

You are where you are because of who we are

Erica Michelle Marie Green that was her name and from all accounts she was a cool little girl, she was pretty, sweet and had a smile that could light up a room but we will come back to her later

If I ever have the chance to talk with our children who have become angels I will tell them that they are where they are because of who we are

We must be capable of expressing the same remorse, the same feelings of anger, the same pissed off expressions that are invoked when we think of the lost little ones of the Motherland

How many of the soldiers in those countries that are flashed across our screens are Fathers

I wonder if the next time 2 African men who are Fathers and are enemies because they are from different sects or groups or villages or tribes or worlds or whatever distinction we use to separate ourselves

What goes through their mind when they cannot recognize the victim because of their worldly hate

Do they see or acknowledge their own seed but because of disgust they cannot stop

Someone told me that children are the reflections of their environment so were these children who were raped or killed are they reflections of the chaos around them

I heard this cat in a movie say "you are where you are because of who you are" and I use that phrase to deal with the question

So when these kid Angels are in heaven playing I am praying that this statement is true

When a man who is a Father kills or a woman who is a Mother kills I wonder if part of them suffers, if part of them has to die with the killing of another person's child, whether it's on the plains of Africa or the plains of Illinois or a desert town in Iraq or the streets of Fort Worth how do they reconcile with God

In America when Klansmen killed black boys and girls did any of them ever stop and think that this was another man's offspring that they were mutilating

When pollution from companies that are abusing nature in South America causes the indigenous children of the Amazon rainforest to die because of profit or greed do they at least pause their machines in a moment of silence?

What did those ignorant cats think when they killed Emmitt Till didn't they care that he would never have another holiday, another celebration of his birth

I wonder if we will all have the same remorse for those little white girls from my home state who were killed by one of their Dads

We are so quick to brand the killing as an atrocity, a crime against humanity, we use broad strokes to avoid relating on the most base level

That it's a child, that the victim is someone's hope, someone's inspiration, someone's light was extinguished; In church we sing of how this little light of mine, were going to shine let it shine, this little light of mine we will let it shine

If I ever am worthy enough to get to heaven I am going to tell these children angels that they are where they are because of who they are

That life is better because of their fleeting time, that what they accomplished in a few short years or moments or days or minutes was better than those animals who killed their physical lives ever accomplished no matter how long they stalk this Earth

We miss them but every time an unexpected rainbow appears or a rain shower pleases the scorched Earth or a child is miraculously saved, or a child recovers from a deadly disease it's because of their vigil, see we want to equate mercy and justice with children from certain places, we want to have limited sympathy with those who fit the demographic that we want to express remorse about, that if the child is not from a war-torn background, or an impoverished neighborhood, a place where hope never resided that they are the only ones we are capable of expressing sorrow for and I say God Bless them all and when I get to Heaven I am going to tell them

Erica Michelle Marie Green is Precious Doe and she is now a child angel because of her own family, do we weep the same for this child as we do for Jon Benet who came from a privileged background, I do and if I get to Heaven I will tell them both

They are where they are because of who we are

INNER

Inner Intro

Inner stuff, man this is the stuff that roams through my mind, when I am just writing. If you ever want to know that God exists and works wonders, get up early, watch the dawn and night merge together, chill. Turn off the tv, don't answer the phone, maybe play some soft music, some Joe Sample or some old Aretha and chill. Sometimes I just write and smile and these pieces reflect my inner thoughts. I recall when as a teenager I would ride the El/Subway and have my headphones on and just chill, reflecting on life. Sometimes I recall working at the jewelry store for Mr. Liss, hanging out on a Saturday afternoon, going to the arcade, buying tapes and posters, playing ball and reflecting on the hood and life. Those happy thoughts come back, when I first formulated the thought that I would go to college and graduate, never focusing on the name of the school, only that I knew I would go and finish. Remembering how secure I felt on a Saturday night when we would not go out, and hanging with my Grandmother and Grandfather as Grandfather and I watched Saturday Night Live, Granny rocked in her chair listening to the Gospel station and through it all, life was chill. Those thoughts formulate my inner happiness.

Between the cracks

Between the cracks and just behind the hieroglyphics of
humanity and life I felt a oneness with a galaxy of thought that
was previously absent as I basked in the warm glow of the
teasing moments of spring in April as it flowed to May
I silently whispered to the alter ego that lurked in my
subconscious searching for the victor in an eternal conflict of my
mental faculty
Thoughts rebounded and revolved as a halo of knowledge, a
virtual monochromatic kaleidoscope of ideals, some would even
brand my thought pattern as a constant yearning to prove my
narcissistic ways of thinking were granules of corrupted words
bastardized marriages of nouns and verbs that were not even
subtle hints of the polluted ideas that gloriously celebrated non
subtle remembrances of brain power, those thoughts that go
bump in the night, those thoughts that if were ever brought to
fruition would render havoc and destruction on the youth of my
yesterdays
As I fought what seemed to be an eternal battle for as long as
my moons were eclipsed on this mud ball being flung through
space, I sit in slams and think of the gratuitous rejoinders that
were accompanied by echoes of inadequacy
Echoes of glorious commentary that were never uttered,
incapacitating my imagination as I searched ruthlessly through
molecules of my childhood, grabbing onto life rafts of life that
nullified the illicit fornication of evil deeds ill stares undue stress
creating a marriage of ill contempt that reached for the jugular of
my intellect ridiculously depicting me as a self inducing mental
orgasmic champion of memorized male divine bad writing

Deep pockets roaming over mental landscapes

Poetry/spoken word allows me to use styles that enable one to say/write
things like, Harken to a time not fabled but requested to exist
again in dreams, I never roamed highways or byways, I walked
concrete paths, swung from steel bars
Exorcised demons on asphalt battlegrounds, cognizant life
choices
Misstep and fall off like were living on a reality-based precipice
But yet and still for those days of yore I reminisce
Days of subways where I loved the way that I downed the
cholesterol and fatty foods that probably coagulated my system
but which helped to generate my teenage wisdom which
allowed me to stay afloat while less equipped friends were not
able to cope
Word
Words were like gold that I found in the mines of life and which
provided me not with just material wealth but mental and
spiritual wealth
From some days and Sundays of sitting on the front pews
listening to the Reverend reverentially spread the news of
salvation
While outside the refuge of the Lord it seemed my world was a
conflagration of sorts
Good thing I was able to resort to
Words
Words that contained the memories that I was able to garner
while traveling on trains and by ways around my home
residence, the words that reflect the times that when we placed
plastic mats on cement
And began to spin on legs and arms seeking to charm the fly
girls of our local world
Saved by these
Words

Ever Briefly

Ever Briefly she touched my imagination as she expressed
views that I had long held sacrosanct and
was convinced no one else would recognize them
She reached out through fiber optics and held my hand and
soothed the rebellious teen not to pacify
the spirit but to simply say "its awright"

She modulated her tone giving me a lifestyle glimpse that
provided me with a reason to continue our
conversation late into the night
I cracked a door on long shut thoughts that had grown covered
with cobwebs in the corners
of my mind

But she now cleaned some of the debris from the surface of my
soul and helped me to polish it to a
high gloss gleam
I moved, I ran, I walked, I stood still, and I ran to standstill as
her mother wit and charm shone down
on me like a benevolent and warming sun

And she did this ever so briefly

Inner Workings

Really I have no idea why God blesses me with these words,
why I am a writer, why I do what I do
My mind races and I acknowledge that there is nothing new
under the sun; we are all just spins off the old,
but these words jump out of my soul at times, and they force me
to write, Man, it calms me down, makes me hype, makes me
high, gets me drunk on these words; Baby it's real
I recall days of yore
When the trip to Kankakee was anticipated by meetings with
family and endless joy in Pioneer Park
It seemed half my childhood was spent at Redwood Inn or
walks down by the Frank Lloyd Wright House on the banks of
the Kankakee River
Midnight trips across the yard and playing the Price is Right as
we all laughed at Let's Make a deal
Black and White Flash Gordon, wrestling featuring Dick the
Bruiser
As I sit in glass towers forever reaching for the platinum ring I
escape back to home with a mere thought

Midnight Hours

She works
A simpler but nonetheless truer line, the sister works
Now some work to achieve to brag
Some work to achieve a higher meaning, some work to escape
the insanity of life
But this woman works because she understands that in her
DNA is the mark of an achiever
This sister works because she realizes that the financial gain is
good, the prestige is cool, the recognition is fine, but the steps
on her walk are intrinsically tied into who she is

Work known by any name and is the same, whether it is called
effort, labor, employment, anything it is known by it is still work
So her efforts at current vocation and her position are directly
related to her laborious and continuous success at her chosen
employment profession

There we have defined work, but we have not begun to define
who this woman is, she sets the average, she is the bar, she is
the threshold, she is the gold standard, the one others watch
The one others whisper about, the one others simultaneously
envy and admire
They know she does not rely on her past achievements, that
resting on her laurels does not exist in her world
That leading by example is not just a corporate mantra on a
poster, that all those fluffy sayings and all the hyperbole
amounts to nothing when you are sitting in the midnight hour,
working not for the satisfaction but because it satisfies your soul

My Resolution (for my mentor B. Fran)

My resolution is revolution so slow down
I resolve to revolt from myself and let the inner man rejoice in
freedom by destroying my self-inflicted shackles of doubt and
ignorance linked together by a chain of selfish acts
I find myself walking through the brightest darkest hallways of
my mind walking down corridors littered with the carcasses of
my failures, I encounter portals that transport me into a realm of
being where successes lie behind a fragile barrier
But every time I move towards breaking the barrier the enemy
appears to block my path, so I turn and I flee and I dive and I
dodge and I escape the enemy by finding solace
In a room entitled Temporary success
From my ventures I am famished but Temporary Success re-
energizes my cells because my tank is empty I have lost
sensation and watch time slip
But the enemy approaches and I vacate temporary Success to
run into another enclave; I enter a holding entitled Quick
Solutions and in Quick Solutions I notice that I am clothed in
robes of Crimson and Cream, so as I marvel at my garments a
sage in Purple and Gold approaches from the East but my sage
does not use words like harken, instead he uses a phrase that
begins "Dog team, you possess lessons from learning so quit
you're messing and start earning"
The sage isn't raucous but has the force of 10 men with his
words and he tells me to rise as a man stands
So I depart Quick Solutions with my sage but he diverges from
my path and points me to the west
As I turn I hear the enemy approaching and I dodge into a room
entitled Excuses, where I am nearly enchanted by beautiful
fluttering maidens that go by names like Doubt and one is called
Failure and they offer me nourishment in the form of despair
Which entice me to quit my journey when I realize that these
minions and their products are minions of my enemy
So I flee but run out of room as I turn the enemy has me
cornered in reflecting pools that cascade into a lake of
enchantment titled Responsibility
Finally the enemy and I come face to face and the enemy
cannot be defeated because
My enemy is fueled by failure and I realize that the enemy is
ME

The Quiet Hours

I heard this sister say in the quiet of the mind is where people speak the truth
The words that are being formulated, that are being propelled out of our mouths into that vast void we call life are sometimes used to sustain our life buoyancy, keep balance between what we think and what we say

Like in relationships the things that build foundations are the hand holding moments, the times when you both sit, chill, listen to what's not being spoken, that's when that person is with you
If we just stopped talking, at times we could understand what is being spoken later
When a parent disciplines a child it's not the physical whipping that determines their actions it's the inner voice, when they can't see or physically hear the lesson

Recently my man passed away and I was sitting in a quiet place imagining he was in front of me, jive talking, wise cracking, bragging about music, life, love and friendship
When I realized what Preach said in Cooley High was so apropos "Cooley high days"

As I continue on this leg of my journey, sitting by myself but I'm never lonely, because in those quiet moments I call my Grandparents name, I recall my long gone friends, I re-think of those fun times with my departed family, I remember how I recoiled at the lessons I was taught at that time and how they now serve me well

We teach that it is calmest before the storm, that we attack at dawn, "walk softly and carry a big stick", I choose to believe the lesson of how in the quiet moments my Creator approaches me and teaches me, that in the midnight hour I learn, that in the stillness of the morning delivery is assured, I choose to sit and reflect and smile to myself I am communing with my personal saints, we are in a cipher of our own

In my neighborhood we use the phrase "yo, you see what I'm talking about" as if we could draw you a mental picture, but it's just an invitation to quietly think about what we are being told, what we are trying to relate, life lessons

We also use the word peace, which to most is the opposite of war, the opposite of calamity, of chaos, the refuge we seek from the inner conflict

I was told when you are doing right and quietly going about your business is when people talk about you, and they talk loudly, and they look for faults in the glare of the day or the shock of night but when you quietly go about your business, your quietness is strongest

Quiet, solitude, life, a child is born screaming but death is silence, but what if death is not silence but peaceful celebration of a mission well done, goals achieved, races won

Now the same sister told me when people watch you walk away the thoughts in their mind is what's reigning true, when I leave this mike, my thoughts will remain, the validity is not at question, the importance is not debated, the aim is to have you chill, go into your inner-being, and achieve peace with yourself

Saturday afternoon

I met her on a Monday morning but when I saw her it turned into a Saturday afternoon
I mean it was like instant relaxation, the world glowed when the young lady slowed and showed reciprocal greetings upon the initial meeting
See she was like a delicacy to be enjoyed, incredible upon the hand touch
Where my hand she touched like shock to my system
For me a Saturday afternoon is special and therefore I likened her to that day which I felt like God had made just for me
I imagined that God had decided that instead of 24 hours in a day he was going to extend it forever
Deciding that morning would flow into afternoon and we would not have a night again
See because the morning starts out as a promise of glories untold, and afternoons are the fulfillment of that promise
But night signifies that the day has to end and after consulting with God he had decided that Saturday afternoon would be forever
Saturday afternoons are reserved for listening to John Coltrane
Saturday afternoon are reserved for lunch at outdoor cafes playing Al Green
Saturday afternoons are reserved for listening to Shuggie Otis or the Brother Johnson's interpretation of Strawberry Letter 23
And like them I begin "Hello my Love I heard a kiss from you
And use them to conclude "Rainbows and waterfalls run through my mind" Saturday Afternoon has never been so divine
And I ask God to bless murky Monday mornings so they can all turn into Saturday afternoons
So from now on I rename her Saturday afternoon
Because those afternoons are reserved for afternoon lunches with your crew,
Reserved for lounging, for letting the ignorance of the work week cascade off like dirty water
If I had to answer as to why God created Saturday afternoons, it's simple, that day and time is the time that we mentally cleanse ourselves, the time that we metaphysically need to replenish our souls
See Friday night is just got paid time, and Saturday night is go out and create memory time and
Sunday morning is make amends with God time but Saturday afternoon is me time
Her and mine time
And then I begin to recite her name like a prayer, like a

mantra....
Saturday afternoon, Saturday afternoon. Saturday afternoon
so when you see a brother rolling to the J-o-b on Monday
mornings and he is smiling all to himself
whether on the bus, subway or in the ride
He's probably smiling on that murky Monday morning because
to him it's Saturday afternoon

Sitting on Breaker

As I sit here contemplating this journey that we call life

I am faced with choices that most never imagined existed

Dealing on plains that have no name and are ever shifting

Facing challenges in the eye every day only to realize that those are not the true challenges but something else

As I sit on breaker thinking of all the things I have seen, the places I have been, the people I know,

I am faced with a reflection of a person that has found out that I know nothing but yet I know it all

The power of the N word

There is this word that I was taught which has many different
meanings
Sometimes it has 6 letters and sometimes 7
No not justice or liberty, but you can also use those words to
evoke powerful reactions
I am talking about a word that begins with an N and ends with
an R
See it has it roots in two of the romantic languages
In French it comes from Negre and Spanish Negro meaning
roughly a dark-skinned person

But let me give you 10 quick examples of the usage of the word
1. If you an African-American cat sees a good friend on the
corner he may walk up slap palms and say "what up my nigger"
2. Now contrast that with a person of a different ethnic group
who sees a black guy do something he does not like he may
also call the same guy a "nigger" but the reaction is, somebody
may then call the ambulance
3. Like if you see the movie Shaft and Richard Roundtree is
kicking behind man we may say that's one tough "nigger"
4. But see a brother who spends more money on his car and
accessories and he lives in his Momma's basement of a
dilapidated house we say that's a stupid ass "nigger"
5. If read about a brother or sister in corporate America taking
game from the street to where the white collars meet, we say
that's one smart ass "nigger"
6. But if we see 4 or 5 sisters standing around at work who
arrive at 7:59 and they start at 8 and they take a 15 minute
setup time, and 15 minutes to get their coffee and 15 minutes to
call their husband, man, girlfriend mother or whomever and then
another 15 minutes to gossip around the water cooler and talk
about everybody else we say they are engaging in some old
"nigger mess"
7. If we hear of a public official who takes every opportunity to
downgrade or denigrate their own people and refuse to stand
up, and whenever a tough decision comes along they side with
those who do not have our best interests at mind or who get
television and badmouth affirmative action or want to cancel it
out and act race neutral we say that is one sellout "nigger"
8. Or like when some segments of society see sports stars and
they don't equate them with the same neighborhoods that they
refuse to walk through and they only talk about them when
referring to crime rates, some of they think in their minds that
those sports stars are ok because they are one of their "niggers"

9. Or when certain officials badmouth minorities in this country in certain quarter's people say wow what a "good nigger"
10. Finally look at those people who like to see the whack rap videos because they love to see the dancing "niggers"
There you have it 10 ways to use the word nigger, now as for me, they can have their niggers because I am hanging out with my people

The restaurant

On the Westside of Chicago and on the streets we call the Low End our people from the south settled there

They came up after the promise of the 1960's not aware that jobs in the steel industry would soon dry up

Not aware that jobs in the land of promise would soon not be there

They had families; they had children who were either toddler or who were raised in the North with no sense of the South

With no sense of where Mom and Dad came from

Mom and Dad did not have much beyond a grade school graduation, not much beyond a basic education

They suddenly went from winding roads and friendly faces to winding roads of subways and exhaust fumes

They spoke English but with a southern drawl so strong, using euphemisms, ethnically speaking that their brand of English, their command of English was foreign in their native land

And their kids, their kids were isolated; they were in a poor environment, parents overwhelmed and under prepared, and scared

The kids were teased because Moms and Dad to their peers talked like no one else

So the kids turned to their support system found on the streets

The gangs convinced these kids of American foreigners born in the U.S.A. that no one would help them

That no one could help them

So the kids joined the gangs and sought protection

Dad turned to the streets, turned to the bottle, all his promises, all his dreams gone up as he tilted the purple bag

Moms at a lost, dreaming of home, wishing for home, saying it would be better back home

And the kids, the oldest son has to be the man that his Father was in the south; he has to protect the family

So he hit's the streets and he fights, and he never quits because little sister is real cute, and little brother got a big mouth, and Moms gotta work, and Pops he gotta continue to believe in himself

Big brother realizes that it is up to him to protect them all, he is the guardian of Momma's dream of home, he is the champion for little brother, the fighter for little sister and the support for his Pop

In order to stay on his mission big brother must politic, he must network to protect his family, and so he meets the streets at the restaurant

Once there he meets with an ill crew you see at the restaurant is where he hangs out, because he can no longer eat Moms and Pops slave food, that soul food, ham hocks is swine, and chitterlings is evil swine, and ox tails is for monkeys

But at the restaurant he eats fried burgers and French fries for breakfast, and at noon he has another fried piece of meat, and at 6 p.m. he has a fried snack and late night more fried food before he retires as he continues to fry his soul and mind

But the restaurant can't replace Momma's soul food, you see soul food just ain't good for the body, it's nourishment for the soul, you see soul food is prepared by Momma's hand, bought with Poppa's hard-earned money, full of the nourishment of pride, fortified by hope, consisting of generational ties of those who persevered to bring them to that time and place but you can't get this in the restaurant

At the restaurant the cats play the dozens and make fun of his Moms dressing for that slave job as a maid downtown, and his Pops finally got a job as a janitor's assistance in a tenement, and they are now considered poor instead of dirt poor

At the restaurant big brother learns the lessons of life as he is forced to accept the fast and furious lifestyle of the city or the soul food loving of down home, so he embarks on a quest to leave the restaurant

The slavery of freedom

What's amazing in this day and age of high-tech access to ever
material dream we can have, how we are enslaved by the
freedom of imagination
For instance if someone dreams that they are a big music star
and they have no discernible talent, all it takes is the
manifestation of the dream of convincing people you are
talented
Don't believe me "American Idol proved me right"
Ever dreamt of bringing scorn and revenge on an enemy who
threatened a family member
Iraq is a testament to a dream of getting the person who
threatened dear old Dad
Ever imagine that you can look like one of Hollywood's or
Madison Avenue's idea of beauty and you have no bucks
Well guess what? You are in luck check out "Nip and Tuck"
Ever thought about fronting to the world that you have lots when
you live on a shoe-string budget?
Gotta love it, cause you can put precious metals on your teeth
And now mere Indians are chiefs
Ever imagine that material possessions could be such a social
weapon and that the bigger the better and that if you mortgage
today and tomorrow
You too can be an oversized SUV and be the envy of the block
But who cares that you have no money in the bank, dodging
bills
Cause you are the cat's meow, you are the one that the world
admires
We have the freedom to treat people real, but instead we
critique those who don't even have the right hair texture on their
heads
Good hair, bad hair, bald-head, dreds, color permed
This is the slavery that freedom has helped us earn
Now name brands have a game plan that show the more
ridiculous and expensive
Our freedom slavery becomes more extensive
5 letters cost five hundred dollars, Fendi, Gucci, Prada
5 freaking letters and we think we are better than the next man
Who said freedom is symbolic of those who are free and dumb
I too am a hypocrite because a bald-headed cat from the North
Cack-A-Lacka
Had me buying his sneakers, even though at that time
I should have been elevating my mind

When rocking mikes we have the choice to be free from rhyme
schemes and categories but yet we revert to tried and true
proven word play grooves to mentally move
The freedom of slavery to a religion that was used to subjugate
and used to hate
We now embrace
Christianity, Islam, Catholicism whatever God or entity you
believe in all has ups and downs but yet we rush headlong
To spend money for material trappings to broadcast how we are
better
I never knew that it cost so much financially to worship God and
that the joy of contributing to something to some person who
has motives we are not sure of
Told us that if you give me a check God will bless you, instead it
seems to me it stresses us out, so is this done to curry a
minister's favor or to impress your equally sinning neighbor?
The slavery of freedom

Who I am not

I am not that six foot something curly haired aquiline nosed wealthy icon that the media tells you to love, and admire
I am not that big broad shouldered cat who can relate to you stories of being a thug, of running from the police for crimes real or imagined
I am not that man who went to the correct college, who hangs with those you admire
I am not the one with the rims on my car, with the large expensive house, or massive bank account
I am not the esteemed Neo-Soul Bohemian with the oh so perfect dredlocks, espousing the virtues of little known artists or avant garde peace movements, I am the cat that you mentally label as one who blends into a background of static noise
One who cannot possibly have an imagination and cannot appreciate an independent woman such as yourself
One who your friends and contemporaries avoid because I look oh so ordinary, because my hair is curly but not curly enough, I am cool but not cool enough
But what you don't know and will never know is that I am the one that will stand not like the Rock of Gibraltar but like a man
I may not have a lot of material wealth but I cherish every thing I have earned
When those other cats that you admire pass you by as you run to them for attention realize they cannot appreciate you for you and I shall not be there
I am the one that shall inspire true life legends of perseverance, of dedication of service to our community
I do not hate those mentioned prior, for they are my friends, my brothers, my frat, my compatriots and for every ten of them, there is one of me holding it together so they can be our artisans so they can help plot the next move, I am standing guard so that they can dream and help us to imagine a better time in our lives
But you my sister refuse to see it, refuse to acknowledge a man who hides in sunshine, a man who has to work that nine to five so others can party forever, that I am the hammer that we call on to assist with change
Next time you are out strolling and you pass the garbage man, the teacher, the hourly worker, the cat without the corner office, realize you may have just passed your blessing

HEART MURMURS

Heart Murmurs Intro

Heart murmurs, the things that make me think on past, present and future relationships. Things that I did not think about, things that I experienced, things that helped me define who I am as a man, as a brother, as a lover, and God willing as a husband, a member of our community, maybe as a Father, maybe one day someday but for now things that make my heart murmur.

2 Kisses to a Promise

Poise, grace, wit, variables of a lady in my presence that made me contemplate who exactly was she
I thought to myself in her unadorned Saturday regalia she has the air of royalty the realness of an around the way girl, and the smarts of true mother wit tempered with true knowledge
I began to think that this lady could be the prize, the true reaching of what it means to be real, the essential element in a concoction of a life that was in need of a missing ingredient
I mean I knew that she was not perfect and that I wasn't perfect and that's what made it so perfect
So I had to dig deep, and control myself from reaching across a wooden table in some cheesy strip mall joint and grasping her cheeks and looking into those beautiful eyes and
Kissing her
Little did I know that I would soon avail myself of the want to touch her lips to mine while discussing the effects of slavery on our present generation
While dissecting the juxtaposition of why our people do not strive and why we suffer from twin maladies of ignorance and of competing with ourselves
for the latest greatest gadgets and then front on ourselves
Little did I know I would kiss her in the shadows of a wonderfully dying day that I have not experienced in ages
The very next day after attending my partners leap into life with his chosen lady, while on my way back to the place where I rest my head, I dropped by
I stopped by with the wrong brand of ice cream in tow as a make-up gift for a little fuss we had
When I damn near had to control myself from a desire to grab her beautiful legs and
But wait I digress, because just thinking of her in those cut off shorts is making me a little stressed and we cannot have that thought on the jay-oh- bee
Or can we?
But instead I got a second kiss
This led to a promise from me to her, or her to me, that we shall be real
with each other
And all this from a desire to kiss

Dedicated to Boom X

Politics to politricks advance from capitals to capitols to capitalize
those who capitulate
In the name of capitalism as they capsize the boat
And de-emphasize the vote
Used to play sentry for what the white landed gentry wrote
Bringing death in the form of presents
Treating some citizens like peasants
Its evident we get kicked by donkeys and can never ride the elephant
Submission of secret missions as former prodigies are protagonists
Father to the son but the whole world is dissed
A hierarchy of hypocrites aren't hip to scripts as they dip
Into funds for old ones as they order the death of everyone else's daughters and sons
Democracy to demonic?
To some the leap is just a simple slip of phonics
Race to space while chasing oil like tonic
From political pundits to pulpits
Some want to punk and pulverize those with non-pink skin and non-blue eyes
Some say that the cats and their cronies who ran places like Halliburton
May have the whole world hurtin
Never rode a camel and never want to handle an M-16
And the war I know is on my scene
Ancestors struck and formed the fight for civil rights while beaten and
kicked on picket lines
But now their kids fall in order only for a ticket line
To hear false prophets kick products
Commercialized Kwanzaa and regulated Black History to one month to fulfill
the promise
In only 36 years we went from Dr. King and spawned Clarence Thomas
Politics to politricks are slick as grease
The summation of it all is that the tricks never cease

Existence

Reality, Being
Words that each signify different states that we occupy
Sometimes when life is unbearable and we just try to make it
through each day we just exist, we are just there we are trying
to keep our head above water as the world is inundated with
misery and strife
Or we think of our state before you
Reality
The fact is I faced a reality where it is full of promise and is so
bright I need my shades at noon
But somehow seeing you makes the existence of my reality a
little bit brighter, makes me anticipate at least one smile a day
Being
Finding out that by just being myself, and watching you be you
is exactly what my psyche ordered
Watching this woman create a reality of peace, of tranquility, an
aura of joy creating a reality based on just being herself
Chill
A word that I was taught to just relax and take it all in as I
observe your style and substance and calm invigorating the
spirit with images of you
Finality
Never questioned, never desired never sought but nevertheless
its upon us, the realization that life is to be experienced, to be
treated like a fragile object to be valued like you are to be
valued
Age
Too old to play games, I am still too young to contemplate my
last days, I am too dumb to totally enjoy life
But I am just smart enough to realize that you are special
There we have it my existence and questions of being are not
finalized and my age still allows me to just chill with you

Familiar

I had just completed opening dialogue with this sister who was
as familiar as yesterday and as promising as tomorrow
She spoke with a self-assuredness that did not speak to
cockiness, which did not speak to false bravado
This did not speak to a world weary outlook
But one which caused me to say "do I know you"

We had never spoken verbally, we had never exchanged more
than hit and miss greetings
We had never heard the vocalizations of past memories which
harkened to times in which innocence was accepted,
proclaimed but not recognized
We had never done more than exchange pleasantries but yet
we found commonality

In the annals of life, I had never met her, I have never seen her
But yet I know her

She is as familiar as Al Green is to Love and Happiness
As joy is to pain, as accomplishment is to blood sweat and tears
She was her multiplied in ways beyond the megahertz
She was as familiar as the black keys are to the white keys on
the piano of experience and life
She spoke as if she was that nighttime disc jockey you listen to
on Saturday's when you are out cruising alone with your
thoughts
She spoke as if she was the woman Lionel Richie missed in
Easy Night Sunday Morning
And I found myself asking "do I know you"

I recall listening to "Sara's Smile" and had often wondered what
the woman would look like who had that smile
As she talked I mentally pictured that Sara would be envious
because she may have been the model behind the song
The reason poets write sonnets, the object of songwriters
longing, she may be the reason men strive to attain greater
heights
And yet I pause just to ask
"do I know you"

Have you ever felt trapped?

Have you ever felt like a prisoner incarcerated without any
bars?
You ever look in your partner's eyes and knew that the felling
was gone that the only action greater than action is inaction?
I am talking about the area where you are afraid to leave
because the rhythm of nothingness has trapped you in a
lockstep to meaningful oblivion
Where your every waking moment is spent plotting on ways to
avoid your significant other
Where you devote more energy to being unfriendly but your
intentional, unintentional measures to drive your partner into a
mad frenzy utterly fail
Where you lie there at night with a contemplative look plastered
on your face but beneath it you internally wail
At the night like a wolf howls at the moon
Where when your special person is greeted as if death has
come over for dinner when they enter your room
Have you ever run and ended up nowhere and you are at the
last place you were seen
Same scene, addicted to the mundane routine, where familiarity
breeds not just contempt but cowardice on your part
Where kindness is a gesture and a measure you no longer
enjoy
And where every waking moment is an effort to permanently
destroy
Where you ask the God of our forefathers to release you from
this pit of hell that is masquerading as a relationship between
sentient beings
Asking yourself is this purgatory? Is this the prelude to the Lake
of Fire, is this what it means to be one of the living dead
And then you remember that night when you met that special
someone and you
curse the day that your partner replied to your
Hello

Message from a Soul Sister

I had just broken up with this fly sister and was feeling bad but she contacted me and I want to inform the world that

When she spoke, angels did not sing, traffic did not stop, rivers did not cease to flow
What occurred was 2 adults meeting on common ground
See she was as familiar as the worn leather seat in a 72 Cadillac
When she spoke it was like liquid butter poured on warm raisin bread that you eat on those cold cruel wintry days
While some have comfort food she comforted the soul
I asked her and she stopped me, she told me that true love is not a verb but an adjective
She told me that it's an action, that if you love someone you will sometimes have to walk away from them
She taught me that true love comes in a feeling of guidance that it is a transporter

That when it is done it is like Captain Kirk saying Beam me up Scotty onto a new world
That sometimes it is there only to help you get from one place in life to the next
That she had taken me to that place in life and she was not leaving me because our love had grown stale and withered like a rose on the vine of life but that her work had been done

She said baby I gotta go, she said it's not because you are not a fly brother but K. I have done my job and when you fall in love again I want you tell the next sister

That you have been prepped and prepared for your journey by the ex-sister

That when you recall our magical, mythical, mystical nights build on those with her

That how you used to call me just to say hello call her to say hello and then some

She wanted me to walk the path I had chosen and that the season of us had come and gone but like a favorite childhood memory one that you recall whenever times get rough

This sister was that memory

I looked at her shadow longing for her embrace remembering when we made love long and slow like the turning radius on a Deuce and Quarter

Remember when my name was the chosen name, when my style was her style creating our style

That sister said K you are a good brother and you treated a sister well all day long and twice on Sunday one day you will be that husband, Father, provider, protector so says

A message from a Soul Sister

Mocha Desire

Chilling
I encountered this sister who got flavor, a sister who is chilling,
one whom I look forward to her messages
Have you met someone you never knew but you know she
existed?
That somewhere out there she was there, chilling, just chilling
She told the world that she has average looks but only if beauty,
style and substance combined in one person is average
So many have come my way, some recent, some long ago,
some left me with memories, some good some bad, but this
sister is telling the world that she is Mocha Desire
Mocha is a dark olive brown, desire is a request or petition
So I guess I request that this dark olive brown sister come my
way,
So we can
Chill
See this is a Mocha that Starbucks ain't got on the menu, one
that Seattle's finest cannot touch, one that is honed, and borne
by that sweet down home black flavor
She told me that she works for the ones who bring the power
but the shock and jolt from one of her messages is a thrill itself
Her smile is like a million kilo-watts tripled, her words re
incandescent, I mean the sister radiates like a thousand suns
captured in her smile
And we just chilling
I want to see her, to check her out, see what she got popping in
that region of the world, this sister got mad flavor
Got a desire for higher ed, for better than average for the only
thing average about her is her style
It's the average style for a jewel of the American concrete Nile
Step to her, and see the exterior, get to know her and check the
interior, begin to dig her, and see the soul
And maybe one day I can chill with my mocha desire

She was her

She was aiming for the roof but landed in the lobby trolling with
the rest of the idle dreamers
She was satisfied with making time for flashy things that
dazzled the senses but caused her to forget her rudiments of
life
She had more material goods than earthly virtue but her chorus
of meandering girlfriends told her she was right in every aspect
while chortling out of her presence at her lack of insight into true
character

Her background was one of meager living, of concrete
stairwells, of a single mother who was raising boys when all
around were men who had their dreams as boys destroyed by
the harsh reality of living in buildings thinly disguised as prisons
Her idea of achievement had nothing to do with material gain
but just being able to buy enough to feed Moms and family
Her education was centered on being able to escape on a daily
basis from life in the pro-jays, forget name brand universities,
city college was good enough, working part-time at a
department store and hitting a poetry spot when she can,
sometimes she reads and the bourgeois sisters admire her
natural hair-do and her authentic voice of the ghetto as they
hang out in their expensive vintage jeans so they can look hip
Not realizing her jeans looked old and cool because they were
old and she made them cool
Not realizing that her hair was natural because it was less
expensive than a perm or weave

She and her passed on the way up, one was driven to make the
Executive suite her goal, the other made being a better woman
her goal, and they looked at each other as mirror images
Her and she realized that they were sisters of the dust
One belonged to the leading church; the other belonged to a
store-front house of worship
One was in a sorority of sisters who focused on looks; the other
was in a sorority of those focused on achievement
One danced the night away at the fly spots, the other danced
the night away at reggae joints singing songs of quiet revolution
while grooving to melodic tunes that swayed the mind and
soothed the spirit
She focused more on making sure her spouse fit a paradigm
and equated money and wealth with good virtues
Her spouse was a struggling doctor who had wealth in
knowledge and was kind and gentle but broke

She married a prominent Dr. of Philosophy who was a school administrator and he had a regular golf date on Wednesday and screwed his secretary regularly on Thursdays and on Friday's they and their perfect children were at the country club continuing the charade
Her spouse finally made it, after years of giving back, they finally were able to enjoy life and then
She and her passed on the way at a charity function for urban young professionals they looked in each others eyes, they saw not mirror images, both 42 years of age both with 2.5 children, both with goals achieved, one had the world weary look of chasing a dream that sapped her energy and life as she set goals that in the long run amounted to nothing
Her goals were achieved as she had the look of contentment
Neither sister is wrong for the affairs of the spirit and life, never questioning the journey only the steps along the path
Peace

Still Water

When I met her I had no idea of the level of level of soul she possessed

No idea that she was a spirit that flesh and blood could not contain

Not a clue as to how to relate to a woman who was top shelf, black label

If I had to think of a superlative to describe her that would be it

Super

See I knew she had the poise wit and charm that lesser cats could not relate too

The essence and totality of high character that magazines write about

People fret for, the type of class that parents pray that their children should embody

It was unusual that this lady said that I caught her eye

But I digress for this is not about me, this is about a person who has come to mean friend in every sense of the word

The opposite of pathos is joy; the opposite of uncivilized is Ethos

So this woman's display of ethos brings me great joy

Brings me a smile, a warmth, a feeling of comfort a level of pleasure, a measure of contentment

That I have not experienced since I was young

Again this is not about me, but a woman whose very voice I
have come to equate with wisdom

With humbleness, with respect

The fortune of our friendship is incredible

I feel like the majority owner of stock that started out at two
dollars a share and split and quadrupled and that tripled and
that doubled and now I am the single solitary majority stock
holder in our enterprise of friendship

Stunned, pleased and fortunate to count her as a friend,
knowing that I am proud to say I am a step f her journey of life,
that I can tell the man she will marry that he is fortunate

That she is the epitome of a lady

That her sweet, consistent, unashamed, ways are like still water

Running deep, running strong, and running true

Two of the World

I thought the most erotic thing in the world was when she said
hello
In that moment was captured not just promise but a thought that
I had Nirvana Valhalla, the Fabled Atlantis, all the wonders of
the known and unknown world
I felt had conspired to produce a woman as lovely as her,
That they had gathered together and collided in a positive
manner to compel her to say
Hello
My mind raced as I imagined the wonderful adventure that we
would embark upon,
As I imagined dancing the night away with her in our favorite
reggae club
As I imagined that she and I would walk down Michigan Avenue
stopping for lunch at a hip eatery, going to outdoor concerts,
debating the issues of the day
Visiting on chilly nights warming each other
When she said hello all the X-rated movies in the world could
not ever summon the force of pure unadulterated erotica that
she emitted at that moment
She did not speak it like a vamp, more like a loud whisper
I wanted to tell her that when darkness comes I want to
illuminate our physical forms like fireflies buzzing around the
lantern of life at night, I want to blur the line between fantasy
and present removing my glasses, which provide me with
physical vision but yet as our bodies and souls become
enmeshed my true vision
becomes clear
When she said hello I wanted to tell her that I desired to feel her
embrace and if I am around when the world deals her a blow I
want to kiss away her salty tears
Crash the barriers that would separate me from receiving all of
her affection, I felt like I wanted to see her sleep and when she
rises to venture into the cruel world
I want to caress the indentation that she left where she rested
I want to tell her that
Between midnight and 1 a.m. I shall divide our world into the
continents
Between 1 and 2 a.m. I will form the seas that shall bring forth
the nectar of love
Between 2 and 3 a.m. I shall cavort like a rampaging beast in
mountainous peaks and make myself known
Between 3 and 4 a.m. I shall be an explorer finding unparalleled
treasures as I find new territory in which to establish an outpost

of romance
Between 4 and 5 a.m. realizing that we have nearly formed our
world and that we are competing with the rising sun
And at 6 a.m. we shall acknowledge that our job is done
And all this from hello

You are

It took me awhile to write this, to find the stroke to understand
the vibe
It took something special to realize how special you are

You are what I know but never knew until now
The epitome of it all, my fellow dreamer, you are

I trusted you to trust me, and though doubts may arise, and
issues will happen
Pride they told me as a child goes before a man falls, pride they
showed me as a man can lead to a man's fall
But charity, wisdom, were also lessons I was taught all of which
you are

I sit in midnight hours nearly dwelling in an internal purgatory
and I think of you
I stand on stages in front of strangers exposing my human
fragility living in the glow of God's smile
Taking light taking charge thinking of home, realizing I feel
home even when traveling with you

The road turns twists, doubles back and the ending has not
been written
The uniqueness of you, the qualities that I adore, that I place
highest
Simply begin with, you are

BLACK FOLKS

A Gathering of men

In this day and age, in this time when we really do need a
Prophet of Rage
I ask how about we just have a gathering of men
No not heroes, not those cats who live incredible lifestyles and
are one in a million
But just some brothers who go to work everyday, avoid the law,
and support their families
I am so sick and tired of seeing brothers with super fancy
gadgets and accessories
Who forgo the necessity of just being a Father
Of just getting up in the morning and going to a job
Just making sure that the kids have some decent shoes and
clothes
No, a 5 year old does not need a pair of Air Jordan's and
Tommy Hilfiger shirt to match
And yes I do think it's something a little strange when you insist
on piercing a child's ear to prove a point
By the way getting little Ray-Ray a fake cell phone, really ain't a
good idea, nicknaming him pimp is not the same as calling John
Jack
See I have a simple request to see a cipher of brothers, not
brothers who want to be everything to everyone
Not brothers who enjoy wearing a nylon doo-rag, a ball cap and
a bandana in 90 degree weather
But a brother who goes to a job, not trying to be the man, or
impress some lonely sister in the next cubicle or fronting, but
just working that nine to five
We get bombarded with these brothers who are exceptions
even for white people and we take it as the norm
We believe that we have to live like the whack rappers in the
video's and cheap record covers, of the movies
Guess what Belly was fiction, most cats live closer to scenes
from The Wood
I would just live to see a gathering of black men not confronting
drug dealers and telling them they are evil but understanding
that because older cats did not present options
Slinging rocks became the pastime of the block
That because black men wanted so much to be cool, we
sacrificed our birthright
See revolutions don't happen because we sit in spoken word
joints and say it's a revolution
They happen because so-called average cats decide to ride
For every Malcolm X. we need a soldier, for every Dr. King we
need a marcher

For every A. Philip Randolph we need a porter
What we don't need is another slave to material possessions, or
a slave to his loins
Not every cat who laces them up is going to the NBA or the NFL
or MBL, and not every student is going to have the cure for a
fatal disease
But more of use can have the answer to help us
See I do not need to hear about exceptional brothers, brothers
on the down low, brothers on the above ground, brothers on the
lam
What I would not give for a gathering of men

And here I lie an Ode to Nicole Brown-Simpson

They have demonized my existence and at the same time
immortalized me as being all that is wrong with our system, all
the evils of celebrity justice in America, all that is wrong when a
black man loves a white woman in a world ruined by our
inadequacies magnified under the lights of racist America
They have exploited who I was; they have marginalized who I
am as they propel the twin dynastic values of true sorrow and
exploitation
They on one hand have said our marriage which went awry was
what's wrong with race mixing in this world that a black man and
a white woman can never be civil when their civil contract is
breached and broken
That my death is what happens when one of those darkies gets
out of control
Forgetting I was a victim, forgetting I was once the love of this
man's life, forgetting I was the Mother of this man's children
Forgetting that I am more than a jury award, that I am more than
a cause, that I gave birth to his and mine legacy,
That I am not just a face in a magazine, that I am not just a
convenient victim, that I am not just a reason to seek
vengeance, that I am dead at the hands of ....someone
Whether it be him or someone else, I am more than a monetary
value; I am more than a mere foot note on race relations in
America
I am more than justice delivered or justice denied, I am more
than the revelatory aspects of bad police work, of exceptional
lawyerly skills, I am not just a verdict, I am not just a cause, I am
not just a battered wife, I am not just a settlement to be
satisfied,
I am not just another statistic to be pondered on late night TV; I
am more than sound bites,
I am the representative of this, who had life snuffed out,
I ....am dead
And here I lie eternally pondering when that will be noticed

Black God

What if the world acknowledged that God was a Black
man? I mean can you imagine the scene up in Heaven
Angels walking around with dashiki's on, afro's with
picks in them riding in chariots sitting on dubs
I mean it would be like getting in the ultimate club
and you got St. Peter and St. Gabriel probably sitting
online all buff with rueful grins and you can see inside that
heaven is jumping but if your name ain't on the list then you
can't get in
I mean God has to be a Black man cause who else would
send a message to his man Jonah that he needed him to
put in some work and when Jonah tried to ignore God look
At what happened
See a white God would issue proclamations and reason
but a Black God sent a special taxi, a whale so Jonah wouldn't
have any excuses not to get where he was told, only a Black
God would send his son to this world to get killed and that's a
fact
And when they had that Black revolutionary Jesus up on
the cross he looked down at them and told them "don't worry
y'all in 3 days a brother will be back"
Hell, they still talking about how Jesus thrilled them
all that time when he and his crew were jamming and the liquor
store was closed, only the son of a Black God could turn water
into wine
Think about it who else was close enough to tell his boys
that he was going to politic and they took this boat ride, but the
sea was a little rough and to and fro it began to swing
But Black Jesus just hopped out the boat, walked on
the water turned to his crew and said "it ain't nothing but a thing'
Only a Black God would be able to pull off that feat
You know why woman came from Adam's rib
Because you know a Black God loves soul food
My Black God is so cool who else could have worked six days
and made this perfect world and rested on day seven and tell us
that that day is all about Him
So the next time you are in church and they tell you about
worshipping a white God imagine the reaction if they admitted
that God was a Black man

Cruising For all my Lauren's

Smokey Robinson made that jam "Cruising" just for me, it's
Saturday and were on 111th street near the Hoagy shop
I hear my man yelling "yo K. what's the move for the night" we
laugh and give some dap to each other
Suddenly frowns cross our brown brows as we spy enforcers of
the law looking at us wondering if we are doing hand to hand
transactions
That quickly passes as a slight ripple in the day I see a brown
sister with curves in places that would make a Coke bottle
envious
She makes her way across the street to the Hoagy shop to get
her high cholesterol artery clogging fix I hear and see crazy mad
brothers yelling 'hey Miss Lady, Miss Lady slow your road Miss
Lady and let me kick that blazey blah"
Unlike some of the perpetually angry black women of the world,
this home girl is cool, just smiles, shakes her head, moves on
I observe the scene from my perch on the stoop waiting for my
man Windy City Case to arrive so we can kick it live
It's like whoa as we notice these dred Rasta cats in a burned
out VW van blasting some Buju Banton, some Toots and the
Mytals, as we see past some young gang bangers who are
walking a line of invincible masculinity without realizing that they
are contributing to nothing
That while they are infatuated with false bravado and buying
into the image that real men wear clothing so low their waist
band is dragging on the ground
They need to look around
But hey who am I to tell a cat with a gat, except that while he is
working on his rep
Society is in jeopardy
But my message is falling on deaf ears and must be akin to
someone speaking verbal leprosy
I quickly think back, speaking of back, guess who just came out
the beauty salon sporting pants too small for her youngest
daughter Lanaquesha with a smock on and rollers in her hair
Who in the world told black folks that you should wear house
slippers out in public
As she goes into the Hoagy shop getting cat calls from cats on
the strip I see the daily urban missionaries displaying their
various religious tools to the masses
For some it's the religion of drugs for others it's the religion of
Sundays
You guys know what the religion of Sunday is right?
That's when people act like heathens and fools every other day

of the week but on Sundays let the Minister, Iman, or Priest speak
And they are the holiest of holy, they are the benevolent Muslim, the righteous Christian, and the perfect Catholic
But Monday through Saturday they would stab their own Momma in the back
Funny how we believe that the more we spend on a house of worship the holier the house
How we become materially rich but spiritually poor
This is a fallacy we cannot continue to ignore
Neither can we dispute how our parents of the Civil Rights generation rescued us but helped us to continue to lose the fight
How 2.5 kids and the American dream became more important, how status replaced substance how they rushed to provide the world to us but lost our souls
How so many of my peers believe that an expensive something and a name brand anything provides virtue
How we want to believe that morality is in a Sex in the City lifestyle, how its ok to mortgage tomorrow for the price of today
But hey
My buddy arrives and its time to head back out into the streets and dig life
As we are Cruising

Cyclical living

As she makes her way through the rows of promises she uses
the words she was taught as a child to now bless the child to
help plot the course so the child's desk which she now makes
ready contains the promises of each she teaches

She recalls the time when she began the steps on her journey
both spiritual and professionally
She moves in between each row recognizing the desks as
shuttles of not students but passageways of promises, but stair
steps to plateaus of further achievement

As she stands behind each desk and she prepares the place
from where her new class of promises will begin their
adventure, she cautiously smiles
She optimistically remembers the cycle of her own life the steps
along her path, the journey and the guides that's he
encountered

She remembers the goals that she set, simple goals of her class
of promises
She does not burden them with seemingly lofty expectations
She instructs them in fulfilling simple truths, simple trusts as
they begin their journey into a complex life

She moves down the row of promises renewed each time she
embarks on that journey

Doc

How do you thank a man you have never met

How do I conjure words to thank a man I have only been told about

It's easy to thank an ordinary man, but it's not ordinary to thank a man who did nothing else but be himself

You see Doc was not just a suave sophisticated, cool older guy who suddenly appeared

He is a pioneer and it's hard to recognize pioneers in a era of copycats, of media created heroes

This leader, this living icon, this person who exemplifies all the traits that we tell children that they should espouse too

You see too often we celebrate the people in the forefront, ones that we can readily identify but the next time you see one of those Civil Rights era photos think of the unnamed heroes in the frame and you will think of Doc

When you think of those people who paid the price and we talk about integration, about making a difference think of this man

He endured vile and covert and overt racism as he made his way to the white school to fulfill his calling as a teacher, using education as the great equalizer, believing that the words and the totality of his lessons would help one child understand life a little better

He endured in classrooms and on baseball diamonds

Funny thing how a diamond is made from a lump of coal and when he played on that baseball diamond they treated him like the proverbial coal and just like pressure turns coal into a diamond the pressure of success of pride turned this diamond into an even greater diamond, more valuable than the Hope diamond

So all the stolen diamonds in a De Beers mine will never equate to the value of Doc

From Philander Smith, to the Razorback Referee Hall of Fame to helping bring young brothers into the fold of Kappa Alpha Psi, to Fatherhood to today he is the highest order of a man

You see Doc is what we try to be what our forefathers died to be, what we are told that we can be, from the Delta to the highest peaks of academia to fatherhood to the Deacon board, to whatever endeavor he is a man

How do I thank him for being, for setting the goal so high that we have something to strive for

We hear today of how people talk about the social bombs

But how do you thank a man who not only witnessed the social upheaval but was part and parcel

I sit here writing for my friend knowing that there are no words in any known dialect or language that will ever be able to express what should be noted by the world about Doc

So I salute him and I tell them all Dr. Gaines is a man

Her

"Keeping our heads above water making a way when we can" a simple phrase for a complex time

I mean think about it, we had a show about the projects in the City of Big Shoulders

And the opening line of the theme song dealt with our ability not to drown in troubles

Cabrini-Green, the ghetto, the pro-jays, the sho nuff hood

And in the midst of relating this urban drama we had HER

Thelma was every cat's dream, fine as wine, intellectual, spirited, down for the cause

She was the epitome of the around the way girl that every man needs, wants, desires

As a little cat on the Southside of Chicago we used to dream about taking the el to Cabrini-Green and looking for Thelma

We imagined the Chi-Lites had written the song "have you seen her" about HER

In the words of an old player, she was like cold cash money; valued, respected, and not to be played with

She was so futuristic in her style; she was Neo-Soul before soul had even aged

20-30 years later we got sisters trying to replicate Thelma but what they did not know was that she was just a character on a page that was brought to life by a real woman

I have told you before in Chicago we use the term "you see" to paint a verbal picture, and you have to see the verbal paint strokes that we have of this sister, her TV brother may have been the ghetto Picasso but she was the urban chocolate Mona Lisa and that was dynamite

The actress took those words on those empty pages and gave them fervor, verve

Style, substance so you saw a woman who was a pioneer, a woman who took her craft to a new level, if she did not have a permanent tan the world would be celebrating her talents as being the precursor of a positive role in a non-positive time

We endured gasoline crisis, unrest in our ancestral and new homes, inflation, downsizing and plants closing, across the sea Patrice Lumumba was killed, Marley was stoking flames of revolution via song, while Stevie was creating songs in the Key of Life, and George Clinton was getting us up for the down stroke with a Flashlight, dreams of nice homes were replaced with the reality of drugs to make ends meet as babies had whole families

In her fictional home, gangs raged in housing void of real James Evans', there was an abandonment of us, community was replaced by despair but unification was in collective malaise and expediency in our neglect coupled with a lack of life skills

In the midst of it all there was this imagery of reality, of a fictional character played by a real-life woman, you see Thelma the character could not have the depth and nuances of greatness without Bernadette the woman bringing herself to life

Some roles define people, and some people define roles, and sometimes Our Creator decides to allow serendipity to occur in the universe and a writer creates a role for a real woman

I Love to Hate Black Folks

I Love to Hate Black Folks who sit and can express lessons of cultures from ancient times telling the world of their virtues but they refuse to consider the self-inflicted apocalyptic news of today
For they can tell the other's journey but cannot tell me the journey of their neighbor
I Love to Hate Black Folks who travel to events celebrating heritage and history of predecessors but turn there back on our people who need them on a daily basis
I Love to Hate Black Folks who try to capture the essence and richness of us in a look, thinking wardrobe and attire or slang can define our tapestry of life
I Love to Hate Black Folks who switch lifestyle like it's just an everyday thing
For one of my best friends was gay and we would go clubbing and sleep at opposite ends of the bed not an issue, for you see my friend was so righteous as he had a soul that was unconquered by any
Now I stand and watch people switch lifestyles like they change underwear negating the journey of my friend and my ex-girl
I Love to Hate Black Folks who go to spoken word venues trying to re-create Love Jones while not opening their minds to the artists who are baring their souls to the world
I Love to Hate Black Folks who believe that by looking mean, acting tough, replicating terrible behavior they thinking they are to be admired
I Love to Hate Black Folks who swear they want a partner in life who's a good person only to settle for the superficial
I Love to Hate Black Folks who question my journey but have never walked a mile in my shoes
I Love to Hate Black Folks who collect for charities but cannot extend charity to the next man
I Love to Hate Black Folks who convince black women that the term bitch is a term of endearment and that a black man's main function is to play sports and produce sperm and use the black woman as a sperm receptacle
I Love to Hate Black Folks who can tell me about Jon Benet but cannot say a simple prayer about 2 little black girls from Chicago who are still missing to this day
I Love to Hate Black Folks who can spell Prada but cannot teach the youth to spell no less the meaning of Diaspora
I Love to Hate Black Folks who don't allow black people to live

Rocket Man

Someone told me that family is heredity that it usually consists of blood ties, of shared lineage, commonality of genetics and DNA
Family to me is all that and more, it is that feeling of security when you know that there are those who may judge you but they love you, that they are that group of people who supports you when the world seeks to belittle you, that when the chips are down, and the wolves are baying at the door and the storm is raging that when the friends are have turned into foes you can count on that family
Well my physical family lives in the North, my adopted family lives in Austin
And Tweety was and still is a major part of my family
You see when this metaphysical vagabond found himself in the Promised land of Austin, he was adopted into a clan of writers, and in that clan of writers he was chosen to be a member of another clan of brothers, and in that clan of brothers he was tutored in the ways of being a black man, of being strong, one brother gave him physical strength, one helped him with confidence and one nurtured the soul through music, food and tales of sports
Tweety and I would listen to music, comparing knowledge, he trusted me on many occasions with his sound system and his records and cd's and he would hip me to the latest addition to his collection
We would listen to music and he would tell me that it would be awright
You see you know family is real when they give your nickname a nickname, the outside world billed me as K.A. Williams but to Tweety, and Big Tony I am KAW,
To them I am the kid they love to tease and spirit away and take around, to coach and discuss ideas
To Tweety I was always there for life lessons, to me Tweety was the tutor who taught about forgiveness, and love, and that over some fried chicken, potatoes with onion's and beef brisket I would learn that life is special
We listened to Elton John's Rocket Man, and he would tell me about when he ran track, and how we would read track and field news on the internet, and about how he would still receive the occasional email about how fast he was in college, about the kids he coached
Tweety was my Rocket Man, he told me about torn hamstrings, and how dreams manifest into reality, a reality that we did not

expect, and how friends are special parts of this unexpected but just deserved reward

"Tweety Bird" was a cartoon character a yellow canary but the Tweety Bird I knew was a Eagle, a Hawk, a vigilant man who watched over his flock of family and friends, who was proud of his children, proud of the athletes he coached, proud of life, proud of his family

You see this man was a rocket man, he reminds of the living embodiment of the old quote, aim for the moon but shoot for Mars for even if you miss you will land among the stars

My rocket man Tweety is zooming around heaven with Jesse Owens racing with Icarus against the sun, cooking Fried chicken with Ella, asking Billy about her last song, playing hits for Duke, signifying with Richard, and training 4 little girls from Birmingham to run in heaven's Olympics

Tweety you are one of my heroes, and every time I see a rocket or a star racing across the sky I know it's you peace out to Rocket Man

Tell Nefertiti I ain't got nothing for her

Black Queen Sapphire of the Night your name is so
hypnotic it's melodic
Black Queen Sapphire of the Night your name is so
hypnotic it's melodic
As I practice to say it
Because it is I and I is me, the Brown one, the
prophet of romance, the Sultan of realness
We speak languages that coincide with whatever feeling
we engender
Remember I bathe in our emotions
The bat of your eyelash encapsulates me as I find
myself looking into your brown eyes thinking they are
more valuable than the Hope diamond
I long for moments when your full lips that are riper
than sun-kissed cherries touch mine
Now some cats talk about the modern black woman and
invoke the name of Nefertiti
That's fine for them but I prefer Thelma
Some cats mentally wander about the ancient wives of
Pharaoh, but I see the queen of my scene as an around the
way woman
Someone who knows what its like to struggle who has
some seasoning about herself who can understand what
its like to rob Larry to pay Henry to rob Peter who
you had to rob in order to pay Paul
Someone who can relate to a black man who faces
ostracism in a business world that only wants to make
his continued economic subjugation the basis of there
business
Someone who understands that relationships are truly
like ships on seas of life that ebb and flow with the
tide of the day but that the trueness of the course is
an unbending force
See Nefertiti had servants and ruled a portion of the
eastern world
But in the west Brenda survives, Tawanda and Lisa
reign supreme
For these modern day black women walk with heads held
back and whether they are flipping burgers or raising
there seeds on there own or loving a black man that
does not love himself they provide Mother wit and are
regal in their own right
Not eager to rule but eager to flourish in a land that

bemoans their sight
Nefertiti and those ancient world women walk on paths
where they were carried
But our black sisters who sometimes carry names that
are created by their families and have contrived
meanings walk on paths that a race called the scourge
of the Earth soaked in blood and paved our way from
birth
So when a brother tells a sister that she is Nefertiti
or Cleopatra I will tell him he can have her and I
will say a silent prayer for my modern black woman and
tell Nefertiti I got nothing for her

The Barbershop

I remember when hanging at the barbershop could entail
checking out the hot kid with the newest and sharper drop
How we used to talk yang creating slang the whole world would
use, buying 3 wings for a dollar and a slice of bread, some fries
Eating them and then all the patrons eyes enlarged and the
volume went down
As we watch Serena Williams in that black cat suit
I recall when in the barbershop I verbally traveled in time
experiencing bravery in slavery and universes in old men's
barbershop verses
Like ding, ding the bell rings "oh yeah" it's like a scene from
"Good Times", cause it's the local booster and his name ain't
Lenny
My man is yelling ten dollars for 1 DVD or 3 for twenty
As old men passed the lessons of virtues to the young who are
ably confused
Buzz cut outside view the scene so tight, and eye high school
friends who still make high school ends
Trying to get the same old lame chick's knees to bend, and
reminisce about glory days as I mentally speak to myself
My man's glory days peaked out at seventeen and sixteen years
later he kicks the same tales of woe
But in the barbershop I use euphemisms like "don't see about it
be about it" or in my neighborhood you reply to your guy "don't
meet there beat me there"
In the barbershop the societal corrosion or rather the erosion
closes in on a movement that caused Civil Rights explosions
In the barbershop my man dropped dime and cats looked out
for each other
Like once my man said "yo Zulu stay away from the gas station
cause the local buzz is that they got beef with your cuz"
In the barbershop I learned about Will E. Lynch and in a pinch
my men who walked these paths gave me wholes and half that
formulated my mental outlook on life so now I am duly equipped
to socially flip scripts
When I have a kid he will learn lessons in school but his
education will also come from the Barbershop

POETRY

Poetry Intro

Yo, this is when I just wrote while listening to some Dizzy, some Stevie, some Coltrane, some Jazz Crusaders, some Marley, some Toots, some Run DMC, other poets, sounds of life, these are some of the thoughts from the midnight hour.

Butterflies

Check it there was crew of larvae who morphed into some cool caterpillars but in this crew of caterpillars there was one that stood out
This one caterpillar did not have a black and gray shell or covering this caterpillar had hints of red, and some tints of green and had something about the way it moved
It did not just crawl along at a reduced pace it sashayed as if it was a model at a 5th avenue fashion show

The other caterpillars left trails of where they had been, they left hints of the leaves that they had consumed to help them eventually morph
But not this one, you see this caterpillar had style and verve that the others could only dream about
And when this one morphed it did not just become an ordinary Monarch butterfly, it became one of soul
When this one flew it did not wait until it was warm enough, it did not need a good draft, this one soared
This one did not dip it dove, and when it lit down, it chilled

For you see this butterfly was not just a result of nature it was the essence of all butterflies before and after

Dancing with her hands

Check it, because this sister out of all the others
This teacher out of all the others
Breaks down barriers and enhances cultures while bridging
gaps that are no longer gaps but passageways and she does it
with her hands and feet
She shows those who were blessed with the ability to detect
nuances on a different level, they are not vocal in the traditional
sense, they do not speak in the same cadence as you and I
Their speaking is on a different level, what we use to grasp they
use to communicate
An opposable thumb may be the link in a complex chain of
communication
And she teaches them with all the subtleness of grace
And she teaches them with the entire God given mother wit she
possesses
And she teaches them with all the years of life learning she has
encountered
And she teaches them in a manner that does not pity but
celebrates

She shows moves of a culture born in the Bronx and which now
sweeps the world in a global impacting event
The culture that came from the ghetto and is now celebrated in
palaces
She guides them in the dance that is both prideful and
respectful of a heritage that encompasses cultures from across
the seas that sprinkled their influences in our movements

Some ask is she a guide, is she an advance scout, is she a
modern day sage

And I reply she is a teacher

Microwave Poets

I was reading this quote about how until "the lion writes his own story the hunter will always be glorified"
As I stand and listen to poets who have microwave mentalities, those who believe they are the greatest thing since sliced bread, those who forget where the art form came from, and the only time they quote a prior poet is to invoke the requisite reference to a revolutionary activist
Typically if I could sing this would be the time in the poem I would sing a popular old school song to fill in the gaps where I lack true contextual value
I can't sing but I can paraphrase and if I had a hammer I would hammer out a warning every time one of these poets approach mikes
If appearance could be a substitute for skills every baggy jeans, Converse sneaker wearing, Che Guevara sporting poet would be the only one's we listened too
Microwave poets tell you about the hood and hanging on the corner and the old days of Hip-Hop, they quote obscure revolutionaries
Poetry does not have to be your world, be your all in all, be your thing but respect the art
Microwave poets strike the pose as if they are humble and kick the ballistics about life and they act as if they are teachers, and are humble when standing before a crowd when in actuality a lot of them are prima Donna poets, also known as God poets, they have big movements, they wave their hands as if they conducting a band, they play the role as if they are poet incarnate, they have a tool box of poems, they have a black woman poem, a screw the government poem, a drop out of society because they are hippies poem, they have a metaphorical poem about nothing but they swear they told you something
I am not the best all the time, I am proud, I am not that handsome and I am not too far removed from rocking poetry born on skills of street corners, see I like good old fashioned

poetry that born from street anthems, spiced up with a slice of life in the south, fortified with some northern flavor, and baked in the Texas heat, and it's more fulfilling than a microwave poet ever will be

My friends

My friends are the greatest things since sliced bread
My friends are the illest rough neck crew on the block
So goes the typical sentiment when people speak of their
friends
As for me, my friends are flawed, they bleed when you cut
them, they cry when you hurt them, they sometimes say things
that I don't understand

You see some of my friends are writers, and they write like it's
essential to their living
They create worlds and dissect thoughts as if they were laser
tipped surgical knives slicing through veins to unclog mental
arteries

I have traveled the world over via their words, I have died, and
been resurrected in 10.27 seconds
I have sat blindfolded in a chair waiting for my lover
Been broke, and only had five shots to make one
I have been entertained, skewered and placed in positions that
were totally unattainable
But they are still my friends

You see, they accept my blunders, chastise my failings, reward
my success, provided shelter when needed
When I have children I will pray that they have friends like mine
People who have so much dirt on each other they could
blackmail each other
That my seed enjoy life like my friends, they live life like my
friends, and they exhibit the same pride like my friends
Shadrach, Mechach and Abednago were models of friends; I
mean you can't get any closer than being in a fiery pit going to
your doom and surrounded by friends

Whodini had a jam about Friends and asked, "How many of us
have them, the ones we can depend on"
If they knew me they would know my friends created a crew of
writers, guided by a Hustler and his life partner
They would know that some of my friends know guys who were
looking for that good stuff from here to Harlem
That my friends sing with Mojo and sometimes nod as they
Page Dr. King

See my friends encompass so much via a piece, heck they are so good that one burned and made the whole world Choke as she told them to bury her ashes outside of bookstores when her days are done
We partied with a world-class sprinter as we house partied with spoken word cats from the whole region
Left them desperate for more verses from the R.P.M. when we step to mike's people always going just look at them
We negotiate through shark-infested venue's leaving lesser cats shook
Left them all believing in one thing, that my family is made up of my friends

I am just a poet

One of the most gangster lines I ever read was by this Persian
cat who kicked the ballistics nearly a 1000 years ago
He wrote "take the cash at hand, let the credit waive and heed
not to the rumble of the distant drum"
That's poetry baby, pure poetical a titanic meeting of verbs and
nouns
And it stands in stark contrast to many of the efforts that I hear
from contemporaries
Poets who decide to create greatness, poets who have culled a
following among a clique of non-poets and to whom they
present throw away lines of dramatic nonsense no substance
words of flash and dash, they have managed to create the
verbal version of Donald Rumsfeld's shock and awe, full of
promise but empty as cotton candy, great on initial taste, light
as the air, goes down easy and later we realize how detrimental
it is to our system
Poets who put more stock on creating names of bravado, of
putting forth a physical image of coolness, of being aligned with
those who they have deemed as God poet manifested
I have learned that when you write and you hit that spot, you
have got the groove, you feel humbled and proud, you look at
the page, screen, napkin, your hand, the window, the back of
your shirt and you remark to yourself quietly
Nowadays I hear and see poets who strive not to get better as a
writer but better at slamming, better at being better than the
next one, better at being recognized as being deep, better at
wanting to be worshipped, better at everything except being a
poet
I recall those days and times when I became a Hip-Hopper
striving to get on the mic, those days and times of rocking
shows and having poets tell me poetry does not rhyme, those
hours and minutes of poets wanting me to understand some
archaic perspective those minutes and seconds of being
frustrated because I do not want to be judged but I subject
myself to judgment when I slam and when the slam is less than
honest having beginner poets tell me that's how the game goes
And as I look and I recall standing on corners as the rain gently
fell rocking in hallways to a beat box for a demo tape, paying to
get in talent shows, and running for my life when we won in the
wrong neighborhood, until that very moment as this poet tells
me that's how the game goes

I question myself, why do I write, is it to win, is it to be recognized, as I listen to poets who strive to create lines of memory only to have them be erased as footprints in the sand I know you cannot desire to be remembered by your words, Omar Khayyam wrote the quote and when he did I bet he never wondered about his place in history or memory
He was just a poet

Quantifiable

Measurements of tablets of words sometimes dictate
responses, which are pre-ordained
Consequently we have to sometimes explore depths of
thoughts that we did not foresee
Such as death of real life heroes, birth of real life
children
Elders taught me you rejoice at death and you cry at
birth

I wonder about how the same things that make you laugh
make you cry because both involve life and passage
Used to be adults begot children but now young adults
begot teenagers who begat children
Grandmother used to do the hustle and can remember
being young watching Good Times and Mother can
remember pop locking and now she and her seed can both
quote the latest rap lyrics with clarity
But they lack true vision of life
Time is one thing they say we never have enough of and
yet it keeps running, sands of hourglasses of passages
that we mark not as passing years but as moments of
life

Experience they tell me is one of the greatest
teachers, well if it is so great then why do we see
the same mistakes so either the teacher is false or
the lesson is wasted on the lost
We measure success in titles as we approach committing
social suicidal tendencies creating whole industries
out of producers of feel good pills who may be shills
who send us to a doctor with a couch who we pay to
spout things that convolute our dreams
But what if that doctor does indeed in fact hold the
key to inner recesses that could alleviate our
stresses

Just listen black cause if it's true ?
I'd buy Freud a line of coke
If it would help us all to cope
Life created in a void where incessant dreams invade
my reality and then I confront where and who I am,
looking for a magic wand, searching for a life
affirming revelation

Questing for piece of something to call my own
I'm a virtual vagabond, and on the road is where I
found my home
I find peace in the brown eyes of a special someone
who seeks out a better life
Posing issues and challenges never front the words,
wearing facts like armor, causing cats to reflect on
past misdeeds knowing that what the fly miss needs is
honesty and realness

Feel this
Life escapades cause people to revolve like orbs
around life synomous as the Sun get too close and get
burned
But stay in perfect rotation and its real
Wisdom is like a floatation device, buoyed by truth
floating on the sea of expectations capsize when we
realize that formats are not applicable
But the brown-eyed vixen makes her presence felt by
the spirit of her movement by the words she speaks
Me thinks we seek down earth homilies to pose answers
to queries that speak truth
See the vitality of life is proof

So we cease then resurrect thoughts that were as
dormant as the half-dead
Now my better mental half once said that
The quest is better than the culmination of the trip
Finding peace in her arms and blessings on her lips
Can't rescue me or recuse me or excuse me from
answering the issues that I have rung
Speaking to the satanic rituals that some worship and
Some call life

I have danced on pin heads, got mentally drunk with
the physically inebriated, walked through the world's
brightest tunnels funneled knowledge like contraband
nuggets of soul and been told
To amount to something one has to reach the depths of
inner being
For the archangel of the all eye seeing is your
conscience
One who can battle himself and self-inflicted inner
demons can overcome any earthly foe or setback
Get back

As we hurtle through space on this mud-ball
It is either illusory or reality that causes us never
to fall
But still I hustle
To reach for rainbows that represent arcs of nihilism
for there is no pot of gold
I only seek to speak and to have a brown sister to
hold
Now that's Quantifiable

Reality fighting dreams

The dream of happiness is as elusive as that midget Irish guy
with a pot of gold
The reality of it all is that happiness is as cosmic as outer space
as real as the soil we played in as kids, as concrete as the
streets on which dreams were first hatched

Sometimes it appears that my dreams of happiness are
scrubbed with the harsh Ajax of reality and what is left is a
sanitized version void of all color, no texture, no flavor no spice,
just flashy gray matter
I recall like yesterday when we met, kissing under the stars,
holding hands on the night I crossed the sands thinking that the
pot of gold rumored to be at the end of the rainbow was actually
found in a brown-eyed woman from a small town

Never forecasting that stormy weather would ruin my refuge
from the life storms we encountered
Someone said do you hate the way things ended, and I no more
hate the ending as I can hate the vision I possess in my
physical eyes, in other words, the journey was worth any
difficulties I encountered

A sister asked me to be honest and admit that I miss my former
friend, and I asked her does a bird miss wind when trying to
gain flight? Did Jordan miss Pippen when trying to win
championships? Yeah I miss her, so look and reflect that
happiness is not controllable by one party or the other, it's a
joint venture, I gained knowledge, saw my strength was above
average, realized I have nothing to regret, that she is a special
person and in a room in my heart she will always reside, maybe
one day the door will re-open but if not that room will remain full
of pleasant memories
Hearts get hurt, but mended, words get stated and sometimes
regretted, when you realize a special person has to be placed
on reserve,
You see my old boss told me in most cases in life there is no
such thing as a permanent friend or a permanent enemy but
permanent interest; this is what happens when reality fights
dreams

WRITING

Writing Intro

Awright, if you made it this far, you probably kind of dig my writing. My writing is fueled by a quiet intensity, an implicit need to take this literal nuclear energy that is harnessed inside of me and put it on paper. Then if I feel the need seek out an audience and rock my piece.

Everyone is truly a writer, life is truly a great play but we have to choose which character we want to play. Will we be the villain? The hero? The goat? What and who are we, and in reality we are all of those characters at one time or another.

My writing is about aspects of me as a black male in America, harkening back to growing up on 111th street, Kankakee, the North side of Chicago, just being a child of the 1970's. I miss the days of Friday night video's of going over Melvin or Brad's and watching video's, then playing ball Saturday morning after cutting the lawn. I miss those times of sneaking kisses in the dark at basement parties, watching the older cats talking to the ladies, seeing the transformation into violent urban scenes. Seeing cats in Roseland, hustling, at Ada Park watching them gamble, smoke dope, talk trash, Sunday school.

Those mental trips fuel my writing.

129

Slam poetry

My Moms told me that one day these two guys went swimming
and one was named truth and the other was named lie, well
truth got out last and could not find his clothes so he searched
for them and could not find them, he ran through the town
straight to lie's house and asked him did he see his clothes

Lie told him that he did not have them well they started fussing
and fighting, and all the neighbors came around and nobody
believed truth because we all know people will accept a well
dressed lie quicker than the naked truth

From street corners to smoky places I spawn thoughts upon
pages and one thought stands out like the bright Northern star,
even though it's millions of thought light years away it's tangible
as now

I cannot stand here and bombard listeners with a piece of
composed prose fake tears, and fake ideas

I cannot sing but my ministry is spoken word, I cannot quote the
gospel but if poetry is religion then I am writing inner city
scriptures

I am writer all day long and twice on Sunday and unlike a Slam
poet I cannot write in a 3 minute burst I create a universe of
thought every time my hands touch a keyboard, or my pen
touches a pad

If being the best at someone else's style is what it takes then I
am not the one, if being overly dramatic and creating the
impression that I am deep then I am not the one

I told them before that my Grandfather told me that deep and shallow are perspectives, that a man can drown in an inch of water and to him that's deep but to a passerby it's shallow

So my perspective is that of a writer who has to slam to obtain silence

To quell the rising of the revolution that is happening in my mind

You see words are building up in my soul and forcing their way out defying me and daring me and telling me that by using them in a piece they can live

If it is words of black achievement that will cause ripples I have those, if it is words that imitate the best rap artists out I cannot construct those, if it is words that move you that are the reflection of another man's style hey I ain't got those

But if it's words of a writer, words of thought, words of a 15 year old cat from the corners, from the Huxtables existence, from the city of broad shoulders words of a man who has more success than failure then that is me

For if "what I am not is exactly who I am", then I don't write slam poetry I just write poetry that slams

So I write

Loud as a street corner preacher
Silent as the hypodermic needle which slips into the arms of
junkies on unnamed too numerous street corners
I flip words like a linguistic acrobat who is walking on a tightrope
of life with razor blades of reality strapped to his soul
My name, well my name is as important as the name of the
Unknown Soldier, in other words representative of the sacrifices
made but yet his payment will never be credited to his account
of life
Who am I, your favorite black guy, ill keeper of thoughts, I host
ideas like honey combs host bees, always searching for the
nectar to deliver to the lair
I walked streets merging with shadows to escape the glare of
the urban landscape, instead of riding with Captain Nemo
20,000 leagues under the sea, I rode 20000 miles on elevated
tracks and subways tantalized not by the song of the mermaids
but of the blind hustler giving out candy and collecting dollars for
his efforts
I remain strong as Hercules, take flight on words like Icarus,
chosen like David but like him I sin, child of the lust, and
champion for those who try to rein in the unjust
My soul brother came from a town known for grilling, outside my
adopted parents house lies my big brother eternally, watching
over me, fast as the sun, he races with the stars
There I go, there I go, and there I go
My words are droplets of water separate just a drip put them
together and the mighty Mississippi is small as a stream of urine
My dream lies on the crest on meadows, I won't settle, but,
when I write I escape the harsh reality, fall into utopia, take a
tour with my Grandparents, point out the sights
So I view life through lenses of glass, physical needed but
maybe the glass impedes my true vision
Janeen Livingston said what if crazy people can detect spirits
and they ain't crazy after all, but they see on a different plain,
because they have a different focus
Should I check into an asylum and get some lessons from those
hopped up, but the drugs don't allow them to exist they might
serve as an anchor to this crazy world
So I write, swift as Hailey's, smoother than Caribbean rum,
strong as Cuban stogies, steeped in the tradition of writers of
life from concrete jungles

I write like Richard Pryor told jokes, I write like a song played by Miles, I write like a sprint ran by Jesse or Tweety, I write like a promise made by God
Loud as a street preacher, silent as the wind, louder than a thought, and a writer by fate

Spitting Dialogue

When I came out the womb I was spitting dialogue
Gave a wink to my Mom's a pound to my Pops and looked at
the doctor and said "what up dog"
Slapped the nurse on the tush because I am able
Threw up the Nupe sign and hopped off the table
Jumped in the buggy cruised to the Hundreds
Got my partners Sam and Dave and we began to misbehave
Went to Kindergarten spiritually nourished at Beth Eden
The life of the Brown one was good, growing up in my hood
Started at Shoop things got hectic
Moms grabbed the belt and found resources to correct it
Ended up at Jahn, learned the ways of the world
Being a male black child with different shades of boys and girls
Hip-Hop branded me, landed me in a world I never knew
existed don't get it twisted
See cats went from the 78 to 79 saw gangbanging hanging on
the stoop, wisecracks got me smacks on the behind
Grandfather role model, Pops a role model, Uncles and older
cats role models
Even the pushers and addicts showed me which roads not to
follow
Graduated went to Lane Tech came correct but I cut more class
than Lawnboys cut grass
Morgan Park next greatest school of them all
Ran track saw lifelong friends writing on the wall
Older cousin had a crew took a chance
He told me to avoid the pitfalls and keep my nose to the grind
Older cats stopping shooting ball and started with 8 balls
K Mays Windy City Case gave me my props and helped me
leave that place, played it loose, made mistakes friends got
killed but I stayed real
So I take it back to the block to the days when Crash, Mark and
Darryl parks we rocked
To first concerts, hickies and slugs
Told the whole world that the Wild 100's I loved
School taught me proper words and the so-called world
But so many intellectuals were uncivilized
It seemed in the Wild 100's is where I met the most wise
Some white cats taught me to bring symmetry to my world by
learning from both, so from gangsters to Kings I can quote
Spoken word gave me reason to express my voice
This piece I dedicate to those who gave me freedom of choice

Words

I sit here contemplating, wondering will my peers ever acknowledge that my ideas are nice

I refuse to lose Im amused by the thought that I have to bring the drama but they don't realize that I am both master and slave to my words

See my words recall days of rage when I was 16 and would hold my girls hand as she looked at me

How this super cute sister made the ugly cat feel perfect not knowing that her glance of affection was not about romance but behind her deep chocolate eyes she felt the pain of another brother who sexually abused her, how he sexually confused her how her pleas were cries of please oh no please and how she was eased into a lifestyle of girl on girl love

How I thought it was wrong love but as I saw how happy she was all she wanted was love

And it was my words that helped me through

See I wonder if my peers will dig my ideas which are nice as I recall hanging on corners late night slapping palms, busting rhymes, sweating the fly sisters, asking for numbers, I can't get enough of the street life, of the night life, of the right life, I can't get enough out of life

As I recall yelling black power hanging with my man who's Mom's was white and his Pops was black

So he was bi-racial but our racial nation said it ain't 50/50 because his Pops is black he has a higher ratio but I didn't see that I saw my friend who dug my words

He was my locker partner, my ace in the place, he told people I was so nice with the words except I didn't have any words when he went to our high school and got that and he cocked back at cats who rocked hats in a different direction and my man shot that thang at men who were separated by nothing

I wish my words could have told him popping lead ain't the way, see so many of peers talk about the love of black people but I heard as my man stood there and shot at black people was he torn, was he thinking he could kill half of himself that he would conquer half of his soul

Are these his questions as he sits in a cell wondering what could have been my friend is free through my words

See I wonder if my peers will dig my ideas which are nice because I cannot cry on stage I cannot tell you bout violating a woman on stage I will not tell you white people are devils and black folks are evil and brown folks are taking job, I can only relate the words that traveled in my mind as I rode subway trains late night watching the stars in the sky, how the universe through my words let the sun and moon exist at the same time, my words has the Sun rising in the West and the Moon in the East and the seas boil with promise and the trees are have leaves of hope and that 15 year old boy from the southside is back on the corners rocking his words

Negro

Muslim Imam's have issued a death sentence against
cartoonist's who have depicted the Honorable Prophet
Mohammed as a terrorist
I mean 12,000 Muslima's marched arm in arm protesting the
depiction of their Most Honorable who in a cartoon had a turban
like a bomb
Thus far over 100 people around the world have been killed in
rioting because of these drawings
Now stop and think for a minute if black folks in America reacted
the same way when they hear the word Nigger, think of how we
would we react as we have brainwashed white people and
young blacks into thinking this word is acceptable, recall how
you feel when driving or walking and you hear some of the most
ridiculous rap music and every other word is my Nigger
They have turned the word Nigger into a religion, pretty soon
instead of little black kids praying at night to God you will hear
them uttering prayers that go something like this "My Nigger up
above nobody can judge me my nigga but you, I love you my
nigga, bless my Nigga's cause they some good Nigga's", and
on Sunday morning we go to church where we gonna pour out
some communion 40 ounces for my nigga's who ain't here, and
when they eat they will stack it up and say My Nigga please
bless this food
Imagine the anger you feel when some young white male is
playing this music that is warping his mind because he has
been told we are all just Nigger's variations of Niggers
Imagine the feeling when you see this white person who we
cannot blame or hate for thinking black people are Niggers
when our music tells them it is more important that we exist with
precious metals in our mouths, with more money invested on
our 32 teeth, a car, than we have in our houses nigga what,
nigga who? That it is more important to mean mug someone,
spend hard earned capitol on fun, more important to getting
your shorty some new Jordan's when he can't even spell ABC
Imagine for a moment if spoken word artists instead of fronting
and being fake humble instead of being a Love Jones clone
would actually use their allotted time to say something, to unite,
to realize what is at stake
Imagine if black folks like the Muslim's in the rest of the world
treated radio directors and disc jockeys like the Muslim's are
treating these cartoonists
We would have marches outside of radio stations and record
companies and we would demand their heads, demanding
accountability for their actions

Demanding that they face up to the crime of misrepresentation, that they answer for telling our kids we are just a bunch of niggers; Imagine for a moment 12,000 black women marching arm in arm down the streets of Chicago, Dallas, Atlanta, Detroit, NYC, Houston, L.A., DC, Baltimore praying and singing that they find those who have decided to have the world view us as Niggers

Imagine over 100,000 black men and women dying so we can't be called Nigger, that all the schooling and the all anti-education movements we indulge in would be focused on the eradication of this one word; Imagine having forums, on Oprah, and Montel, and Wayne Brady singing James Brown's "I am Black and I'm Proud" and all the media we admire having shows dedicated to showing people the beauty of black folks

Imagine a sister getting on Maury Povich's show and instead of looking for the ninth guy who could possibly be little June Bugs father saying "Maury I am here to dedicate my child to the movement of being a black male"

Imagine Destiny's Child instead of singing they need a soldier they need a black man

Can you imagine our black ministers on Sunday Morning issuing bounties on those who promulgate hate, those who tell sisters that if they appear in a video in little of nothing she is modeling, who have dedicated an entire network into believing it's all about being crunk, and acting whack, that on Sunday morning in between passing around the collection plates they told us the story of Jesus Christ Black Revolutionary, of St. Augustine, of Constantine, of Ethiopia,

Imagine for a moment if we realized that Nigger is a 6 letter death sentence, how can you get mad at someone else for using the brand your own have shown the world, so as I depart I realize when I get home I will be scanning the internet for stories of black folks who are rising up in quiet rebellion against the word, like those Muslims we would rise up and speak out, and march and demand that we find those who have branded us as niggers

Patriot Acts (A poem In Honor of 9/11, the Middle Passage and Man's continued pursuit of people elimination)

They told me Thomas Jefferson was a great Patriot
I said ok but don't forget Medgar Evers
They told me about Betsy Ross
Cool, but what about Ida B. Wells
See my thoughts percolate like blades of grass grown in fields
nurtured by the blood and toil of our ancestors
So as I stand here and think of the patriots who became martyrs
on 9/11/01 I reflect on the term patriot and who defines it
A patriot is not someone who just wears red white and blue, but
someone who may sport tinges of red, black and green, a hue
of yellow, or maybe some orange and white
They tell us that patriots are men like Thomas Payne
I say don't forget Benjamin Banneker
They taught us about Patrick Henry
And I say mention Amiri Baraka
They tell me that patriots sit in great halls and debate legislation
and how to help society
I tell them I know plenty of old patriots that sit in black
barbershops in corners playing checkers with wrinkled and
weathered hands that toiled in fields to help bring us better days
As they recall an age old time of then that is as vibrant as now,
who watch the younger generations trade the plantations of soil
for the plantations of concrete shackled to the plow of instant
gratification
Every time I see an old black woman or Latino woman who's
past retirement age taking public transportation to work I see a
patriot who is a living martyr
Every time I read about or see a white impoverished farmer
praying for rain to save the crops I see a patriot
They tell us that patriots are those guys who drop bombs and
shoot guns
 But every time I read of a teacher in inner-city America
teaching tomorrow's leaders from books older than yesterday I
see a patriot on the frontline
They say patriots names begin with George
As in George Patton
Or in George as George Washington
I say cool but the patriot I am thinking of who's name begins
with George is George as in George Washington Carver
In World War II we read about General Mark Clark
I say fine but I read about Generals Mark Clark and Fred
Hampton also great patriots who became martyrs

They taught me that a martyr is someone who gives up their life rather than relinquish their belief
So I think of Emmitt Till, 4 Black girls in church in the south, Harold Washington and how they never relinquished their belief for equality and gave their lives willingly or by force for this dream
When 9/11 comes around I think of the saints who were murdered
And I also think of the multitudes of saints who died on the middle passage from Africa to America
I see a patriot every time I see a single young mother waiting on the bus stop with her child's hand waiting on a bus to go the pre-school and then downtown to an underpaid overworked job
So as we sit and contemplate inane freedom slogans and we judge who the true patriots are
Think of some of these real patriots and their acts

Made in the USA
Middletown, DE
21 May 2019